Certificate

GALWAY...ARIES

WITHDRAWN FROM CIRCULATION

This is to certify that

....

has received this
diploma from the
Sarah Webb
'Kids Can Cook
Around the World'
School of Cookery
having mastered all the
recipes in this book

KU-026-078

Sarah Webb

KIDS CAN COOK

around the world

Illustrated by Terry Myler

GALWAY COUNTY LIBRARIES

THE CHILDREN'S PRESS

To my young testers –
Sam, Zoe, Cal and Luan
and to Ben
with thanks to Rena Dardis
for all her hard work

J 121,346 / 641.5123
€7.00

First published 2001 by
The Children's Press

2 4 6 5 3 1

© Text: Sarah Webb 2001
© Illustrations: Terry Myler

All rights reserved. No part of this publication may
be reproduced, stored in a retrieval system, or
transmitted in any form or by any means, electronic,
mechanical, photocopying, recording or otherwise,
without the prior permission of the publishers.

ISBN 1 901737 26 8

Typeset by Computertype Limited
Printed by Colour Books Limited
Back cover photograph: Siobhra Hooper
Front cover flags from left:
Top: Italy, Mexico, China, Japan, U.S.A.
Below: France, Spain, Sweden, Israel, India

Contents

Introduction

Welcome to *Kids Can Cook Around the World.*

This cookery book brings together recipes from all over the world for you to make. Some are well known, such as *moussaka* from Greece and pizza and meatballs from Italy, and some are unusual, such as *latkes* from Israel and *blinis* from Russia – but all are delicious!

I have chosen recipes that are fun and easy to make, sometimes adapting recipes to suit younger cooks. There are lots of tasty sweet things included – biscuits, cakes and desserts – as these are often the most fun to make (and to eat!). Each country is introduced with some facts on the country and what they like to eat. So I hope you enjoy learning a little as you go along.

I found so many delicious recipes when writing this book that I didn't have space to include them all, so watch out for the next book in the series – *Kids Can Cook 3!*

I have given each recipe stars to indicate how hard it is to make.

1 star * means easy,

2 stars ** quite easy, and

3 stars *** a little more difficult.

If you enjoy using this book you might like to get *Kids Can Cook* which is filled with more fun and easy recipes for young cooks. Available from all good book shops at €6.50.

And finally, if you would like to contact me through The Children's Press (address at the front of the book) I'd love to hear from you. All the recipes are tested by young cooks and if you would like to be on the testing panel for the next book, send me your details.

Happy cooking!

Cookery Words

In cooking, special tools or utensils are needed for different jobs, such as peelers and electric blenders. Special terms such as kneading and grating are used to describe cookery skills.

Here are some of the most commonly used words you will come across in these recipes:

Beating means mixing ingredients together to form a smooth paste, using a wooden spoon (and elbow power). If you soften butter first in the oven or microwave, this makes it easier to work with. But be careful; a second or two will do.

Blending also means mixing together, this time with an electric blender. It is the easiest way to combine solid and liquid ingredients (such as bananas and milk – for a milkshake). Use the blender with great care and keep fingers well away. Better still, ask an adult for help.

Creaming. Butter and sugar sometimes need to be 'creamed'. Cut the butter into small pieces and add to the sugar. Mix together with a wooden spoon until light and creamy.

Cutting. Use a sharp knife – *! watch fingers* – and always cut on a chopping board to prevent marking a counter or table-top.

Dicing means cutting into small pieces or cubes.

Folding in. When a recipe tells you to 'fold' one ingredient into another, this means mixing with great care. Beaten egg whites and flour are one example. Take a metal spoon and gently turn the mixture over and over in the bowl. If you 'fold in' carelessly or too quickly the beaten-up egg whites will collapse and you won't get the lightness the recipe demands.

Grating. Ingredients often need to be 'grated' into small fragments. The usual household grater has two to four sides, each giving a different kind of shred, from fine to coarse.

Kneading. When making bread or pastry the dough may need to be 'kneaded' or worked together with your hands. Put the dough on a floured table-top or counter, making sure it's steady. Using your two hands, stretch the dough, then pull it together. Give the dough a quarter turn and repeat, again and again. Keep doing this until the dough is smooth and stretchy.

Mashing. Vegetables such as potatoes and parsnips often need to be 'mashed', or squashed, into a smooth mixture. This is done with a masher. If you haven't got one, use a fork.

Oven thermometer. If your cooker doesn't have one built in, get a little free-standing one.

Peeling. Some fruit and vegetables may need to be 'peeled'. For this you need a special peeler. Hold the fruit or vegetable firmly in one hand and the peeler in the other and peel firmly towards yourself.

To 'peel' a tomato, drop it into boiling water for 1–2 minutes: the skin will slip off easily.

Rubbing in. To mix flour and butter together into small breadcrumb-sized pieces, rub them between your finger-tips to form crumbs.

Scraping. Vegetables with fine skins like new potatoes or parsnips can be peeled more easily if you use a 'scraper' rather than a peeler. Hold the scraper firmly and scrape away from yourself in short firm strokes.

Seasoning. To 'season' means to flavour with salt and pepper or other herbs and spices. A 'pinch' means just that, a little piece pinched between your finger-tips and scattered over the ingredients.

Separating eggs. If you need to separate the egg white from the yellow yoke, break the egg on to a saucer. Place a cup over the yoke, tilt the saucer and catch the egg white in a bowl, leaving the yoke in the cup. Magic!

Shredding means cutting into thin ribbons (usually used for lettuce).

Simmering is a gentle boil. Make sure the liquid does not dry up or overflow and spill out of the pan. Always watch a saucepan simmering on a ring – just in case.

Slicing means cutting into thin slices.

Whisking. Some ingredients such as eggs and cream need to be 'whisked' to put air into them. You can use a manual or an electric whisk. The manual whisk has a handle which is turned quickly. As you use both hands (one to hold the whisk and one to turn the handle), you must make sure the bowl is steady. Stop it slipping by resting it on a tea-towel.

If you have an electric whisk in the house, ask an adult for help to use it.

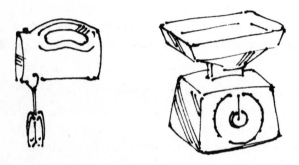

Weighing and measuring. A recipe may not work if you do not measure the ingredients correctly. Use a weighing-scales to weigh flour and other dry ingredients and a measuring jug to measure liquids.

When measuring with a spoon, such as a teaspoon of sugar, the spoon should be level, not heaped.

WARNING! You can't be careful enough when using sharp knives, blenders, scrapers and peelers. Watch those fingers at all times, and, if you use electrical equipment, always have an adult at hand.

Safety First

Safety is important in the kitchen where you will be working with a lot of dangerous kitchen utensils such as knives, and kitchen machines such as blenders.

Top Nine Safety Tips

1) Make sure an **adult** is standing by, just in case. If there is anything you don't understand ask for help.
2) Watch your fingers with sharp **knives** and graters. The edges of cans are often sharp, so dispose of these very carefully.
3) Take great care with electrical **kitchen machines**. Make sure your hands are dry when plugging them in and out or you may get an electrical shock. Never open a blender when it is in use; this is dangerous; and also very messy as the ingredients will splatter out all over the walls and all over you.
4) Never leave the kitchen when the gas or electric rings are on. Always **turn off the rings, switches, knobs or gas** after you have finished cooking. Kitchens can be fire hazards, so be very careful.
5) Have a cloth or kitchen roll to hand in case of spills. Be especially careful to **mop up spills** on the floor, as you or someone else might slip.

6) Always use **oven gloves** or a thick tea-towel when lifting hot dishes out of the oven. Use a heatproof mat or a chopping board to put hot dishes on – these can burn counter or table-tops.

7) Turn all **saucepan handles** to the side to avoid knocking them over by accident.

8) After cutting **raw meat, chicken or fish**, wash your hands, the knife and the chopping board carefully, as these raw ingredients can contain germs. Always store meat, chicken or fish in a secure container, away from other ingredients.

9) Ban all **pets** from the kitchen while you are cooking. They can carry germs and can also get under your feet and cause accidents.

Sorry, Tiddles.

To recap:

Have an adult on stand-by. • Careful with knives.
Careful with electrical machines • Turn off rings.
Wipe up spills • Use oven gloves.
Saucepan handles in • Wash after raw meat.
No pets!

First aid

If you have an accident, call an adult at once. Even small cuts and burns may need a plaster. If the cut or burn is bad, get a doctor or nurse as soon as possible.
Burns: Place the burn under cold water for five minutes and cover with a clean bandage or plaster.
Cuts: Clean the cut under the tap and cover with a plaster.

Before You Start

1 Put on an apron, roll back your sleeves and tie back long hair.

2 Wash your hands.

3 Make sure the work tops and table-tops are clean.

4 Collect together all the ingredients and cooking utensils you need for the recipe.

5 Read through the recipe and make sure you understand it. Ask for help if you need anything explained.

WHEN YOU SEE THE (!) SIGN BE EXTRA CAREFUL

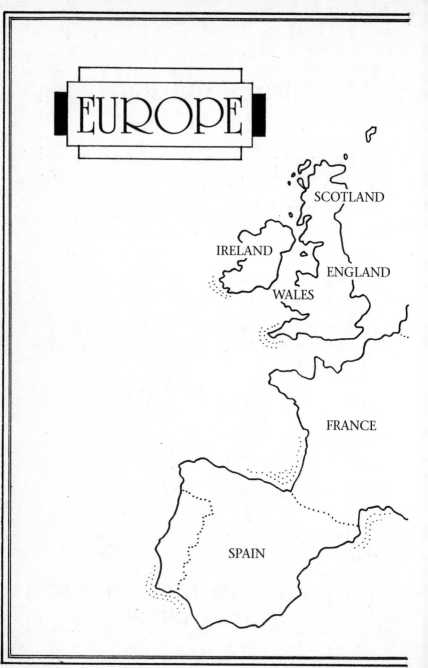

Europe

Austro-Hungarian Empire

The Austro-Hungarian Empire lasted for over six hundred years. At one time it included Spain and the Netherlands and even sent a Hapsburg prince (the unfortunate Maximilian, brother of Emperor Franz Joseph) to Mexico, with the intention to adding it to the Empire; unfortunately the plan misfired and the poor prince was shot. When it collapsed, in 1918, the Empire stretched east to Poland, west to Switzerland, north to Germany and south to the Balkans.

Austria and Hungary were the two principal countries in the Empire.

Did you know: Until the nineteenth century the official language of Hungary was Latin.

*Hungarian Goulash***
(serves 4)

The winters in Hungary are very cold and people want hot nourishing food. The national dish is *goulash*, named after the *guylas*, the cattle herders of the vast plains, who are said to have invented it. It is a hot spicy stew of beef, potatoes, onions and lots of paprika pepper – marvellous when there's a touch of frost in the air. Dumplings, small balls of dough flavoured with herbs, are often added.

1 lb/450g Irish stewing beef
1 large onion
4 large potatoes
2 tablespoons paprika
1 clove garlic
1 tablespoon vegetable oil
1 can of tomatoes
1 beef stock cube
3/4 pint/425ml water
salt and pepper
1 carton of sour cream

Utensils: large saucepan, chopping board, kitchen knife, measuring jug, garlic crusher

---

1 Cut the beef into cubes on a chopping board using a sharp kitchen knife – *! watch fingers.* Meat can be hard to cut, so ask an adult for help.

2   Cut the onion into pieces on a chopping board –
    ! watch fingers. Remove the skin from the garlic
    cloves. Peel the potatoes and cut into thin slices
    – *! watch fingers.*

3   Heat the oil in a large saucepan. Add the beef and
    fry until brown. Add the chopped potatoes and
    fry for another few minutes.

4   Add the onion, tin of tomatoes (juice and all),
    paprika and a large pinch of salt and pepper. Stir
    everything together.

5   Crush the garlic and add to the saucepan. Stir
    again.

6   Boil the water in the kettle and pour into the
    saucepan carefully – *! watch the boiling water.*
    Crumble in the stock cube and stir well.

7   Cook on a low heat for 1 hour, stirring now and
    again.

8   Serve hot with a dollop of sour cream on top.

*Sachertorte****

Vienna, the capital of the Empire, was one of the
great cities of the world, with a glittering court life.
State banquets were splendid affairs with all the men
in gold-embroidered uniforms, the women in de-
signer dresses and the tables set with gold plate and
crystal. Alas, there was one unfortunate drawback.
Emperor Franz Joseph was a man of spartan tastes,
with very little small talk. He disliked lengthy meals.

GALWAY COUNTY LIBRARIES

J121,346.

As he had to be served first and as he only took twenty minutes to eat his meal, the guests were lucky if they got through the first course before he left, thus signalling the end of the banquet.

The hungry courtiers repaired to restaurants, the most famous of which was Sachers (it's still among the top Viennese restaurants). One of its specialities was, and is, *Sachertorte*, a mouth-watering concoction of chocolate and cream which was created in 1832 by Franz Sacher.

This is my version of that world-famous cake.

---

3 eggs
6oz/175g soft butter
6oz/175g caster sugar
6oz/175g self raising flour
1 heaped dessertspoon of cocoa
1/2 pint/275ml whipping cream
1 dessertspoon milk
1 chocolate flake bar

Utensils: mixing bowl, wooden spoon, sieve, dessertspoon, 2 round baking tins

---

Preheat oven to gas mark 4/175°C/350°F

---

1 Place the butter and sugar in a mixing bowl and cream together with a wooden spoon.

2 Add the eggs and beat together. Dissolve the cocoa powder in 3 dessertspoons of hot water and add to the mixture.

3   Add the milk. Sieve the flour into the mixing bowl and fold it gently into mixture.

4   Place half of the mixture in each of the greased cake tins and bake for 30 minutes. To test if it's done, put a knife into the cake and if it comes out clean, it's ready.

5   When the two halves of the cake have cooled, whip the cream stiffly and spoon about half of it on to one half and cover with the other half.

6   Cover the top of the cake with the rest of the cream and crumble the flake over the top. Eat immediately.

France

The Italians claim they are really responsible for French cuisine! When Catherine de Medici (from Florence) married Henri II of France in 1533, she arrived with a team of cooks who taught the French the rudiments of cookery. Whatever its origins, France today has one of the most diversified cuisines in the world, with each region producing its own special dishes. When anyone discovered or invented something of which they were particularly proud, they would name it after the province or town of origin, or indeed the personality involved. Seven names out of hundreds: *Pommes Dauphinois*, *Quiche Lorraine*, *Salad Nicoise*, *Boeuf Bourguinne*, *Crepes Suzette*, *Tournados Rossini*, *Creme Chantilly*.

In France they take food very seriously indeed. The proprietor of one of the most famous Paris restaurants, La Tour d'Argent, refused to serve people who wanted a meal in a hurry (Franz Joseph wouldn't have gone down too well here), and another famous chef hanged himself because the fish didn't arrive in time to be cooked for a court banquet. Not surprising in a country where the chef Escoffier devised 85 different ways of preparing sole and has over 365 varieties of cheese.

Before eating, the French say *Bon appetit* which means 'good appetite'.

Did you know? Mussel farming is said to have been started in the thirteenth century by an Irishman who was shipwrecked on the Atlantic coast.

⌇ *Nicoise Salad* *
(serves 4)

---

2 large eggs
4 medium red potatoes
2 cups green beans
1 head of lettuce
1 large tomato
1 can of tuna
1/4 cup of black olives (optional)
Dressing:
1/4 cup cider vinegar
1/4 cup olive oil
1 tablespoon whole-grained mustard
(Lakeshore or Dalkey)
1/4 teaspoon sugar

Utensils: 2 saucepans, chopping board, sharp knife, serving bowl, small bowl, metal spoon

---

1 Boil the eggs gently in a saucepan for 15 minutes until hard-boiled. Place aside to cool – *watch the boiling water!*

2 Chop the potatoes into quarters. Place in a saucepan and cover with enough water to boil. Simmer for 15 minutes. Add the beans and simmer for another 5 minutes until the beans and potatoes are tender. Drain carefully.

3 When cool enough to handle peel the shells from the eggs and cut each into quarters.

4 Cut the tomato into slices on the chopping board – *! watch fingers*. Drain the oil or brine from the tuna and place in bowl. Using a fork, break the tuna into flakes.

5 Wash the lettuce, pat dry with kitchen paper or a clean tea-towel, and place the leaves in a large serving bowl. Arrange the eggs, green beans, potatoes, tomato, tuna and olives on the leaves. Cover the bowl with cling film and put in the fridge until ready to serve.

6 To make the dressing: put all the ingredients into a small bowl and mix together until well blended. Pour the dressing over the salad just before serving.

Baby Party Quiches **
(makes 12)

Little savoury pastries filled with a delicious creamy egg mix, baby quiches are great for parties. You could also make one large quiche for your family. The most famous quiche is *Quiche Lorraine* which comes from the north-eastern region of France.

4oz/110g frozen packet shortcrust pastry (thawed)
3oz/75g streaky bacon
1 large egg
5 tablespoons milk
1oz/25g Cheddar cheese grated
2 scallions/spring onions
salt and pepper
butter for greasing tins

Preheat oven to gas mark 6/200°C/400°F

Utensils: rolling pin, sharp knife, mug or
circular pastry cutter, 2 patty tins (6 'holes' each),
or one large pie dish (12 inch), frying pan, mixing
bowl, fork, kitchen scissors, chopping board,
wooden spoon, tablespoon.

---

1 Roll out the dough on a floured work or table-top
   to about $1/2$ to $1/4$ inch thickness. Remember to
   flour the rolling pin too or the dough will stick.

2 Cut the dough into circles with a mug or cutter.

3 Grease the patty tins and place one pastry circle
   in each. If the pastry comes well over the top of
   the tin, cut off the extra using a sharp knife –
   ! watch fingers. Put the pastry filled tins in the
   fridge to chill for about 15 minutes.

4 Cut the rind off the bacon with a knife or scissors
   and cut into strips about $1/2$ inch long. Cut the
   scallions into thin slices – *! watch fingers*.

5   Place the bacon in a large frying pan and carefully fry for 8–10 minutes until it begins to turn brown.

6   Beat the eggs and milk together in a mixing bowl. Add the cheese, scallions and bacon and stir.

7   Fill the pastry cases with the mixture.

8   Bake in the over for 15–20 minutes until the egg is set and the tops of the quiches are golden.

Pommes Dauphinois **
(serves 4)

---

2 lbs/900g potatoes
$1/2$ pint/275ml milk
$1/2$ pint/275ml double cream
1 clove garlic peeled and crushed
salt and pepper

Utensils: potato peeler, chopping board, kitchen knife, kitchen roll, saucepan, metal spoon, oven-proof dish, measuring jug

---

Preheat the oven to gas mark 6/200°C/400°F

---

1   Peel the potatoes with the potato peeler. Slice into rounds, as thin as possible, on a chopping board with a kitchen knife – *! watch fingers*. Dab the slices dry with some kitchen roll.

2   Place the milk in a saucepan, add the potatoes carefully and bring to the boil. Simmer with the lid on for 10 minutes.

3 Add the cream, garlic and salt and pepper to the mix in the saucepan and simmer gently for 10 minutes, stirring now and again.

4 Remove the potatoes with a slotted spoon and place them in layers in an over-proof dish.

5 Pour the sauce over them and bake until the liquid is absorbed.

Germany

German food is simple and hearty and eaten in what often seems alarming quantities. Pork is the favourite meat, served in a variety of ways – pot-roasted, in a spicy sauce, made into a loaf with beef, cooked with beans, cured or smoked. There are endless varieties of sausages *(wurst)* and the original frankfurter came from Frankfurt.

After a good breakfast which includes cold meats, Germans begin to feel a little peckish about mid-morning. This slot in the day is called *brotzeit* (bread-time) and doesn't just mean bread. You are not a true *Munchener* (a native of Munich) unless you have eaten *weisswurste* (a white sausage made of meat flavoured with herbs) and drunk a glass of beer before eleven in the morning.

A substantial lunch means you'll probably last out until late afternoon when you can drop into a coffee shop for *kaffeetrinken,* when the true *schwarzwalder kirschtorte* (the Black Forest cherry, chocolate and cream cake) will be on the menu. Thus fortified, you can start thinking about dinner!

Christmas is a very special German festival. Not only does it mean Christmas trees, cribs, candles in every shape and size and wonderful tree decorations, one more beautiful than the next, but all households have special baking programmes for fruit loaves, cakes, biscuits and marzipan fruits. At home I always bake *zimtsterne* Christmas biscuits while Sam tries his hand at a traditional *pfefferkuchenhaus,* a gingerbread house.

Did you know? Many German restaurants have 'communal' tables which you can join if you are on your own. A great way of getting to meet people!

Bavarian Pork Chops *
(makes 4)

---

4 pork chops
1 small onion
1oz/25g butter
1 tablespoon Worcester sauce
3 level tablespoons soft brown sugar
1 teaspoon mild mustard
3 tablespoons ketchup
2 tablespoons malt vinegar
1/4 pint/150ml water

Utensils: frying pan, sharp knife, chopping board, wooden spoon, oven-proof dish, mixing bowl, metal spoon

---

Preheat oven to gas mark 4/180°C/350°F

---

1 Chop the onions into small pieces with a sharp knife – *! watch fingers*.

2 Melt the butter in the frying pan and add the onions. Add the pork chops to the pan and cook until brown.

3 Place the remaining ingredients in a mixing bowl and stir together with a wooden spoon.

4 Put the chops in the oven-proof dish and pour the sauce over them. Cover and bake in the oven for 40 minutes.

5 Remove the cover carefully (always use oven gloves and get an adult to help you) and cook for another 20 minutes until the chops are tender.

6 Serve with mashed potatoes.

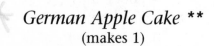

German Apple Cake **
(makes 1)

---

1 lb/450g cooking apples
1 egg, beaten
2oz/50g butter
2oz/50g caster sugar
3oz/75g plain flour

Utensils: apple corer, sharp knife, chopping board, saucepan, mixing bowl, wooden spoon, large baking tin or oven-proof pie dish

---

Preheat the oven to gas mark 6/200°C/400°F

1 Peel and core the apples and cut them into thick slices – *! watch fingers*.

2 Place in a saucepan and add just enough water to cover them. Add some sugar to taste (about a dessertspoon).

3 Place the cooked slices in a pie dish and allow to cool.

4 While the apple slices are cooling make the cake mix. Cream the butter and sugar together in a mixing bowl using a wooden spoon.

5 Add the beaten egg and mix together. Mix in the flour and beat the mixture until creamy.

6 Spread the cake mixture over the apples. Bake for 30 minutes until the top is golden and crispy.

Delicious served with lashings of whipped cream or ice-cream.

Zimtsterne (cinnamon stars) **
(makes 12)

These are traditional German Christmas biscuits which are hung on the Christmas tree. You can decorate them with icing sugar and silver balls or cake sprinkles.

9oz/250g ground almonds
9oz/250g oat flakes
3 egg whites
12oz/350g caster sugar
juice of 1 lemon
2 tablespoons cinnamon
a handful of flour

Utensils: mixing bowl, fork, baking tray,
wooden spoon, pastry brush, rolling pin,
star-shaped pastry cutter, skewer

Preheat the oven to gas mark 6/200°C/400°F

---

1 Beat the egg whites in a mixing bowl with a fork
   until stiff. Add the sugar and lemon juice and stir
   for about ten minutes. Put aside 1 cup as a glaze.

2 Mix in the other ingredients and work into a
   dough with your hands.

3 Put some flour on a clean, dry work surface or
   table-top and on the rolling pin. Roll the dough
   until it is 1/4 inch thick.

4 Cut the dough into star shapes using a pastry
   cutter. If you don't have a cutter you could make
   small rounds using a cup or try cutting star shapes
   with a sharp knife – *! watch fingers.* Make a small
   hole at the top of each biscuit with a skewer.

5 Glaze and bake for 10–15 minutes. Cool on a wire
   rack. Thread thin ribbon through the hole.

Pfefferkuchenhaus ***
(makes 1)

This gingerbread house, straight from Hansel and Gretel, is a little tricky to put together so you may need some help – but it's well worth the effort.

It would make an ideal, and very original, birthday cake.

2oz/50g butter
4oz/110g caster sugar
4 tablespoons treacle
1 lb/450g plain flour
1 teaspoon bicarbonate of soda (bread soda)
1 teaspoon cinnamon
1 teaspoon ginger
$1/2$ teaspoon salt
5 tablespoons water
a little butter
a little extra flour
4 tablespoons icing sugar
a little water
(or tubes of ready-made white icing)
stiff paper or thin card to make a pattern

Utensils: scissors (for the paper), 2 mixing bowls, wooden spoon, sieve, rolling pin, cling film, fish or cake slice, baking sheet, cooling rack, kitchen knife

---

Preheat the oven to gas mark 4/175°C/350°F

---

1   Using a scissors, cut out the gingerbread house patterns in paper or card, following the diagram instructions opposite – *! watch fingers*

2   Cream together the butter and the sugar in a mixing bowl using a wooden spoon.

3   Sift together the flour, bicarbonate of soda, salt, cinnamon and ginger into another mixing bowl.

4   Add a quarter of the flour mixture to the butter and sugar mixture and a third of the water. Continue adding the flour and water until all are used up. Mix into a dough.

5   Place some cling film over the dough and chill in the fridge for 30 minutes.

6   Roll the chilled dough on a clean, lightly floured counter or table-top using a floured rolling pin. It should be about $3/4$ inch thick.

7   Place the paper patterns on the dough and cut around them. You may have to roll the dough into a ball and roll out flat again several times to get the right shapes. (If the paper seems to stick to the dough – put a little butter on the paper first before placing it on the dough.)

8   Cut around the patterns with a sharp knife until you have 2 roof pieces, a back, a front, 2 sides and a door – *! watch fingers.*

9   Using a fish or cake slice, carefully lift the pieces on to a greased baking tray and bake for 10 minutes.

10 Place on a rack to cool before putting your house together. Join the pieces with icing sugar. For invisible joins – melt some sugar in a saucepan and use this as 'glue'.

11 Decorate your house with icing 'snow' on the roof and on the walls.

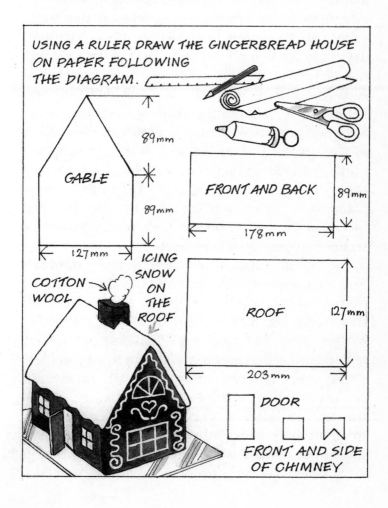

USING A RULER DRAW THE GINGERBREAD HOUSE ON PAPER FOLLOWING THE DIAGRAM.

GABLE

89mm

89mm

127mm

FRONT AND BACK

89mm

178mm

ICING SNOW ON THE ROOF

COTTON WOOL

ROOF

127mm

203mm

DOOR

FRONT AND SIDE OF CHIMNEY

Great Britain

Though the term 'Great Britain' to describe the countries of England, Scotland and Wales dates from 1602, each country retained its own national identity, with its own regional cooking.

In upper-class houses, eating was on the grand scale and the menus from Georgian and Victorian days indicate a lavish life style. Most of the food was home produced from the estate farms. Walled gardens and large green-houses provided fruit and vegetables for almost the entire year. South-facing walls and borders were used to grow early vegetables as well as the first apples and pears. Those facing north ensured supplies for as long as possible through winter and spring. Early peas were particularly prized and the race to have the first melon of the season on the table resulted in fierce rivalry between head gardeners.

The middle-classes also ate well (judging from *Mrs Beeton's Cookbook*, first published in 1859). In the slums, the poor eked out a hungry existence though they seem to have devoured vast quantities of oysters; as a character in a Charles Dickens book remarked, 'Oysters and poverty seem to go together.'

The industrial revolution of the early nineteenth century saw huge changes and, sadly, knowledge of the old traditional ways of cooking was lost. Even though the growing British Empire introduced new ideas from abroad, with Indian curries (Mrs Beeton gives several recipes), Chinese Sweet and Sour, rice and pasta, not to mention unfamiliar spices and exotic vegetables like aubergines and avocadoes, British food lost its quality and individuality. The fast-expanding population was only interested in one thing – cheapness.

Reading old cook-books, I feel nostalgic for once-popular dishes like Grassy Corner Pudding, Candied Cowslips, Scalded Cream, Crimped Cod and Snow Eggs (described as 'A Very Pretty Supper Dish'). However I won't be giving you the recipes for some other famous specialities such as Haggis, Pease Pudding or Jellied Eels – I've never met anyone who likes cooking or eating eels! Instead I've chosen recipes from the field in which the British Isles have always excelled – baking.

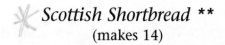 *Scottish Shortbread* **
(makes 14)

4oz/110g plain flour ¾ cup
2oz/50g cornflour over ¼ cup
4oz/110g butter
2oz/50g caster sugar ¼ cup
salt
a handful of flour

Utensils: mixing bowl, sieve, wooden spoon, knife, chopping board, rolling pin, baking tray, circular metal cutter or cup

---

Preheat the oven to gas mark 3/165°C/325°F

---

1   Sift the flour, cornflour and salt into a mixing bowl.

2   Cut the butter into small pieces and crumble into the flour mixture (clean fingers!). Add the sugar.

3   Place the shortbread dough on a floured counter or table-top and roll out using a floured rolling pin until it is 1/2 an inch thick.

4   Cut round shapes using a cutter or a cup.

5   Bake in the oven for 25–30 minutes until golden. Cool on a wire rack.

Bread and Butter Pudding *
(serves 6)

3oz/75g butter
9 slices of fresh white bread, crusts removed
4oz/110g mixed sultanas and currants
grated rind of 1 lemon
3oz/75g demerara (light brown) sugar
3/4 pint/425ml milk
2 eggs

Utensils: oven-proof dish, saucepan, kitchen knife, 2 mixing bowls, wooden spoon, fork, measuring jug

---

Preheat the oven to gas mark 4/175°C/350°F

---

1   Butter the oven-proof dish well. To do this use the butter wrapper or some butter on a piece of kitchen roll or tin foil.

2   Butter each slice of bread on one side. Cut each slice in three – ! *watch fingers*. Place half the bread over the base of the dish, buttered side down.

3   Mix together the currants, sultanas, lemon rind and sugar in a bowl and sprinkle over the bread. Place the remaining bread over the top of this, buttered side up.

4   Put the milk and eggs in a mixing bowl and beat together. Pour over the top of the pudding, cover with cling film and leave for an hour.

5   Remove film. Bake in the oven for 40 minutes, until the pudding is a pale golden brown.

6   Serve hot with custard or cream.

Welsh Cakes *
(makes 12)

8oz/225g self raising flour
4oz/110g butter
3oz/75g caster sugar
3oz/75g currants
$1/2$ level teaspoon mixed spice
1 egg
2 tablespoons milk
butter for frying

Utensils: mixing bowl, wooden spoon, small bowl, fork, circular pastry cutter (3 inch) or cup, frying pan

---

1   Place the flour and butter in a mixing bowl and rub together until the mixture looks like bread-crumbs (make sure your hands are clean!).

2   Add the sugar, currants and spice.

3   Beat the egg with the flour in a small bowl using a fork. Add to the mixture.

4   Mix together until you have a firm dough. Roll out the dough on a clean, lightly floured counter or table-top until it is about 1/4 inch thick.

5   Cut the dough into rounds using a cutter or cup.

6   Heat a frying pan and place a knob of butter in it. Cook each round on a low heat for about 4 minutes each side, until golden brown.

7   Eat warm with butter or cream and jam. Yum!

Greece and Turkey

Greece and Turkey form part of the Balkan Peninsula. Both have had their heydays; Greece when Athens was the centre of civilisation, Turkey when Constantinople was the capital of the Byzantine Empire. Cooking in both countries is rather similar, based on olive oil, herbs and spices. Fresh vegetables are important, either in salads or stuffed. And sweet cakes and desserts, made with honey in Greece and with a syrup of sugar, lemon and orange-flower water in Turkey, are popular everywhere.

The Balkans are sheep country and the Turks devised a rapid way of cooking the meat – *shish kebabs*, which translates as 'roast meat stuck on a skewer'. Pieces of lamb are marinated in oil and herbs and alternated with slices of tomatoes before cooking over an open fire.

Aubergines are highly prized. A famous Turkish recipe is called *Iman Bayeldi* (The Priest Fainted). Some say it was because he liked the dish so much; the other explanation is that he fainted because of the size of the bill. My favourite aubergine recipe, *moussaka*, comes from Greece. It takes some time to prepare but it's well worth it. It's a good choice for a family dinner – so invite the whole clan over for this deliciously cheesy dish. You can use all aubergines or all potatoes but I make it with a mixture of both.

In Greece many restaurants are called *tavernas* and people sit outside, under hanging vines, and nibble *meza*, tasty little bites that come before your meal.

Did you know? The Greeks were probably the first people to record recipes; Archestratus, a poet from Gele who lived around the year 330BC, made trips to other countries to find out about their food.

˅ Greek Salad *
(serves 2–4 as a main dish)

6oz/175g Feta cheese
6 tomatoes
1 small cucumber
1 medium red onion
2oz/50g black olives (optional)
4 tablespoons olive oil
salt and pepper

Utensils: sharp knife, chopping board, salad bowl

---

1   Cut the cheese into small pieces – *! watch fingers.*

2   Cut the tomatoes into quarters and then into eighths on a chopping board – *! watch fingers.*

3   Cut the cucumber into $1/4$ inch slices and halve each slice– *! watch fingers.*

4   Cut the onion into rings and halve each ring – *! watch fingers.*

5   Place the cheese, tomatoes, cucumber, onions and olives in a salad bowl. Mix together. Add a pinch of salt and pepper to taste.

6   Pour the oil over the salad just before serving and toss gently.

Moussaka ***
serves 6

1¹/₂ lbs/675g minced lamb
2 onions
1 tin tomato purée
1 aubergine
1 lb/450g potatoes
1 tin of chopped tomatoes
1 clove garlic
olive oil
salt and pepper
3oz/75g grated cheese (red or white Cheddar)
cheese sauce (use a packet)

Utensils: chopping board, kitchen knife, colander, frying pan, oven-proof dish, wooden spoon, potato peeler.

AUBERGINE

Preheat the oven to gas mark 6/200°C/400°F

1   Cut the aubergine into thick slices on a chopping board using a sharp knife – *! watch fingers*. Place in the colander and sprinkle with 1 tablespoon of salt. Leave to drain for an hour and rinse with cold water.

2   Place some olive oil in a large frying pan and heat gently. Add the minced lamb and fry until brown, stirring all the time.

3   Chop the onions – *! watch fingers* – and add to the pan. Fry for a few minutes.

4   Add the tomato purée, salt and pepper.

5   Place this mixture in the bottom of your oven-proof dish.

6   Peel the potatoes and cut them into rounds (not too thin) – *! watch fingers*. Cook them for a few minutes in a frying pan until they start to turn brown.

7   Place them on top of the meat mixture.

8   Fry the aubergine for about 10 minutes and add the tin of tomatoes and the garlic. Cook for 5 minutes.

9   Add the aubergine mix to the oven-proof dish.

10 Make the cheese sauce and pour it over the top. Sprinkle grated cheese over the top. Bake for 60 minutes and serve hot.

Stuffed Tomatoes **
(serves 4)

---

10 medium sized tomatoes
1 lb/450g minced meat
2 chopped onions
$^1/_2$ cup uncooked rice
1 cup olive oil
chopped fresh parsley
1 teaspoon sugar
salt and pepper

Utensils: sharp knife, chopping board, 2 mixing bowls, metal spoon, baking tray, saucepan

---

Preheat the oven to gas mark 4/175°C/350°F

---

1   Cut a slice from the top of each tomato using a sharp knife – *! watch fingers*. Keep the tops.

2   Scoop out all the insides of each tomato (the 'pulp') and place in a bowl. Put 2 cups of the pulp into another mixing bowl and add the meat, onions, rice, parsley, sugar, a pinch of salt and pepper and half the oil.

3   Cook for 10 minutes in a saucepan over a moderate heat.

4   Fill each tomato shell with the mixture and put the tomato 'top' on each. Add the rest of the oil to the remaining tomato pulp. Salt and pepper and pour over the tomatoes.

5   Bake for 90 minutes. Serve with a Greek or green
    salad and crusty French bread.

    *You could use green or red peppers instead of
    tomatoes.*

Italy

Like Germany, Italy only became unified in the
nineteenth century, so there was never a national
cuisine. Each region had its own special dishes. As a
rough guide, it's rice in the north, pasta in all its
shapes and forms through the middle, pizza around
Naples, fish by the sea, sausages and salamis inland,
especially in the mountains.

There are so many different types of pasta that it
would take pages to list them all. A short list for
beginners: *spaghetti, fettuccine, rigatoni, tortellini,
tagliatelle, macaroni, penne, cannelloni, lasagne, ravioli,
linguine.*

Spaghetti must always be cooked *al dente*, which
means it must be slightly firm, not cooked into a soft
mush. The most famous pizza is *Pizza Margherita*,
named after the first queen of a united Italy.

Though the borders are a little blurred by now,
Italians tend to eat their own local dishes; they
would never dream of ordering *risotto* in Sicily or a
pizza in Venice. And what a roll-call of famous
regional specialities they have: Parma ham or
prosciutto, Lucca olive oil, veal cutlets *alla milanese,*
spaghetti *bolognese,* steak *alla fiorentina*, lamb *alla
romana*, cassata *alla siciliana*, liver *alla venziana*, *pesto*
(basil sauce) from Genoa.

All Italians eat lots of fresh fruit and vegetables (raw, grilled, baked or stuffed), love savoury breads, and think (probably rightly) that Italian ice-cream is the best in the world.

Did you know? In Sicily – where it comes from – cassata *is not an ice-cream; it's a sponge cake with layers of soft ricotta cheese and candied fruit.*

Pizza Margherita ***
(serves 2)

Base
6oz/175g plain flour
1 teaspoon salt
$1/2$ teaspoon caster sugar
1 tablespoon olive oil
1 teaspoon dried yeast or
1 sachet of easy-blend yeast
4 fl oz/120ml warm water
or
1 ready-made thin and crispy pizza base
a little extra flour (cornmeal – polenta if possible)
Topping
12oz/350g tin of chopped tomatoes (drained)
3 teaspoons of fresh basil (or 2 dried)
8oz/225g Mozzarella cheese in slices
4 tablespoons freshly grated Parmesan cheese
salt and pepper

Utensils: large mixing bowl, cling film, wooden spoon, sieve, measuring jug, rolling pin, chopping board, kitchen knife, baking tray.

1   Sift the flour and sugar into a mixing bowl and then add the salt and yeast.

2   Make a 'well' (a hole) in the middle of the mixture, pour in the water and the olive oil.

3   Start mixing together with a wooden spoon and then, after a little while, use your (clean) hands. If you find that there is flour left around the sides of the dough, carefully add a little more water and mix again.

4   When the dough is mixed, place it on a clean, floured counter or table-top. Knead the dough for three minutes using your hands (see instructions on page 10), until it becomes shiny and smooth. (You may find that bumps start to form under the surface – don't worry, it's just the yeast!)

5 Place the dough in a mixing bowl, cover with cling film and leave it in a warm place for about 30–40 minutes, until it has doubled its size.

6 While the dough is rising, preheat the oven to gas mark 8/230°C/450°F.

7 Place the dough on the floured (with polenta if possible) counter or table-top, knead it for a minute or so and begin shaping it into a large ball. Roll out the dough with a floured rolling pin until it is about 10 inches in diameter. Stretch it out another few inches with your (clean) hands, working from the centre out. It doesn't need to be a perfect round shape, just get it as thin as you can and leave the edges slightly raised. Now it's ready for the toppings – pheew!

If you have a ready-made base, start here!

8 Spoon the tomatoes on to the pizza base and spread to within 1/2 inch of the edges. Sprinkle a little salt and pepper and the basil on top.

9 Place the Mozzarella slices on next and then sprinkle the whole lot with the grated Parmesan. Carefully drizzle a little olive oil over the top and bake for 12–15 minutes, until the cheese starts to bubble.

✓ *Penne with Tuna* *
serves 4

---

2 fl oz/50ml olive oil
1 garlic clove
8oz/225g mushrooms
1 small red pepper
8oz/225g tin of tuna in oil
1 lb/450g penne pasta
salt and pepper

Utensils: 2 saucepans, kitchen knife, chopping board, mixing bowl, fork, serving dish, metal spoon, garlic crusher, colander

---

1   Cut the mushrooms and the pepper into thin slices on a chopping board – *! watch fingers.* Crush the garlic clove using a garlic crusher or chop finely.

2   Heat the olive oil in a saucepan on a low heat and gently fry the mushrooms, garlic and peppers for a few minutes, until tender.

3   Put the tuna into a mixing bowl, with its oil. Break it into flakes using a fork and add it to the saucepan with the vegetables. Add salt and pepper and stir gently for a few minutes on low heat.

4   While the sauce is cooking, put the pasta into a large saucepan of boiling water – *! watch the boiling water.* Cook, following the directions on the packet (usually about 10 minutes).

5 Drain the pasta with a colander and pour it carefully into the saucepan with the tuna mix. Stir together and serve. (If your saucepan is not big enough, stir the sauce and pasta together in a serving dish or mixing bowl instead).

Bruschetta *
(serves 2)

Bruschetta is delicious toasted bread with garlic and olive oil. A tasty snack or great as a starter before pasta dishes.

---

4 slices of thick white bread
1 clove garlic
olive oil (extra virgin if possible)
4oz/110g grated Parmesan cheese (optional)

Utensils: chopping board, kitchen knife

---

1 Peel and cut the garlic clove in half – *! watch fingers*.

2 Toast the bread on both sides and rub immediately with the cut cloves of garlic.

3 Drizzle a little olive oil over the top of each piece.

4 If you like, you can add some grated Parmesan and grill until it bubbles.

Spaghetti with Lamb Meatballs in Tomato Sauce ***
(serves 4)

This recipe has three different steps and takes time to prepare. But it's well worth the effort!

Meatballs:
1 onion
1 clove garlic
1 lb/450g minced lamb
1 egg
1 tablespoon dried mixed herbs
1 tablespoon olive oil
Sauce:
1/2 pint/275ml *passata* (sieved tomatoes in a jar)
2 tablespoons fresh basil
1 clove garlic
salt and pepper
12oz/350g spaghetti
grated Parmesan cheese

Utensils: mixing bowl, wooden spoon, chopping board, kitchen knife, baking tray, frying pan, spatula, large saucepan, colander

---

1   Chop the onion into small pieces – *! watch fingers*. Chop the garlic as small as possible or use a garlic crusher – *! watch fingers*.

2   Put the onion, garlic, lamb, mixed herbs and a pinch of salt and pepper into a mixing bowl. Add the yolk of the egg. Stir together until blended.

3   Divide the mixture into about 20 pieces and roll in your (clean) hands to form meatballs.

4   Place the meatballs on a baking sheet and cover with cling film. Place the baking sheet in the fridge and chill for 30 minutes. This is important as it will stop the meatballs from breaking up when you are frying them.

5   Meanwhile, chop the basil and garlic for the sauce – *! watch fingers*.

6   Heat the olive oil in a frying pan. Put in the meatballs carefully – *! careful of the hot oil*. Fry them for 10 minutes, turning now and again, until they are brown.

7   Add the passata, basil, garlic and a pinch of salt and pepper to the frying pan with the meatballs and bring the whole mixture to the boil. Cover with a lid and simmer for 20 minutes until the meatballs are tender.

8   Cook the spaghetti in a large saucepan of boiling water (follow the instructions on the packet). Drain carefully and place on four large plates.

9   Spoon the meatball mixture over the spaghetti and top with a sprinkling of Parmesan cheese.

When you taste this you could be in Italy!

Ireland

Ireland's cuisine relies to a great extent on the best of raw ingredients – beef, lamb, pork, salmon, seafood and fish from the seas around – simply roasted, stewed, grilled or poached.

I have given lots of great Irish recipes in *Kids Can Cook;* here are some more, one based on our national vegetable – the potato – the others on the fruits that grow so well here.

Did you know? Mayonnaise was invented by an Irishman – General Mahon who served under Napoleon.

Potato Cakes **

(makes 8)

---

6 potatoes
2oz/50g plain white flour
2oz/50g butter
1 egg
salt and pepper
knob of butter for frying

Utensils: potato peeler, saucepan, potato masher, knife, small bowl, fork, mixing bowl, wooden spoon, rolling pin, frying pan

---

1   Peel the potatoes, cut into thick slices – *! watch fingers* – and cook in boiling water until soft. Drain and mash until smooth – *! watch boiling water and steam.*

2 Melt the butter in a small saucepan. Beat the egg in a small bowl with a fork.

3 Place all the ingredients in a mixing bowl, season with salt and pepper and mix together.

4 Sprinkle flour on to the counter or table-top and on to the rolling pin. Roll out the mixture into a rough circle a quarter of an inch thick. Cut into 8 triangles.

5 Place a knob of butter in the pan and fry each side until golden brown, 8–10 minutes.

6 Serve hot with butter.

Fraughan (Blueberry) Muffins **
(makes 12)

I first came across this recipe in Maura Laverty's *Full and Plenty – Traditional Irish Cookbook*. The muffins sounded so delicious I simply had to try them!

Maura Laverty was a writer, journalist and story-teller as well as being a great cook. She died in 1966 but her recipes still live on.

8oz/225g plain flour
1 teaspoon baking powder
4oz/110g caster sugar
$1/4$ teaspoon salt
2oz/50g butter or margarine (soft)
1 cup of fraughans (blueberries)
1 egg
$1/4$ pint/150ml milk

Utensils: sieve, mixing bowl, wooden spoon, muffin
tray

Preheat the oven to gas mark 6/400°F/200°C

---

1 Sift the flour and baking soda into a mixing bowl
and add the salt.

2 With a wooden spoon, mix in the butter until it
has just blended with the dry ingredients. Don't
worry if the mixture is now a little lumpy.

3 Add the fraughans, the unbeaten egg, and the
milk, and stir gently until the ingredients are
mixed together and the flour is moist.

4 Grease your muffin tins with a little butter and
fill each two-thirds full.

5 Bake for 25 minutes until they are golden on top.

Gooseberry Fool **
(serves 6)

When I was a child, we lived in a house which had
loads and loads of gooseberry bushes in the back
garden. My two sisters, Kate and Emma, and I used
to pick the gooseberries and eat them raw. They were
very bitter and if you ate too many you got a tummy
ache – but we still did it.

Gooseberry Fool, defined by the dictionary as 'a
creamy liquid of stewed fruit with cream' is a *much*
better way of eating them. You can also 'fool'
rhubarb, strawberries and raspberries.

1 lb/450g fresh gooseberries
12oz/350g sugar
8 fl oz/250ml fresh cream
1/3 cup water

Utensils: hand-held food mixer (or food processor), large saucepan, wooden spoon, sieve, metal spoon, serving dish

1 Put the gooseberries into a large saucepan and add the water.

2 Simmer them for 5–10 minutes, stirring all the time with a wooden spoon.

3 Press the cooked gooseberries through a sieve, using the back of a wooden spoon. If you have a blender, put them into it and whoosh for 30 seconds.

4 While the gooseberries are still hot, stir in the sugar. Chill until cold.

5 Whip the cream using a hand-held food mixer or a food processor.

6 When the gooseberries are cold, fold in the whipped cream carefully.

Netherlands

If you're into art and go into any picture gallery in the world, you'll find – in the Dutch room – lots of pictures termed 'still life'. Usually food. Splendid arrangements of game, fish, vegetables, bread, nuts, pyramids of fruit. No doubt about it! The Dutch love food and eat heartily.

Among their favourite foods: soup and stews, cheesy dishes (there are two native cheeses – the yellow-covered Gouda and the red-covered Edam), breads of all kinds and cakes. At one time Indonesia was colonized by the Dutch and this gave them a taste for eastern food which survives in the *rijsttafel* (rice table) – a big bowl of rice is placed on the table and surrounded by lots of dishes of meat in various sauces, eggs and vegetables.

My recipe is for one of their favourite ways of cooking new potatoes.

Did you know? On the Feast of St Nicholas, 5 December, the Dutch serve spiced biscuits in the shape of the saint on horseback.

Roly-Poly Potatoes *
(serves 4)

1¹/₂ lb/675g baby new potatoes
2oz/50g butter
3 cloves garlic
1 tablespoon chopped chives
4oz/110g Dutch cheese

Utensils: shallow oven-proof dish, garlic crusher, chopping board, kitchen knife, tin foil, metal spoon, cheese grater

Preheat oven to gas mark 5/190°C/375°F

1 Wash the potatoes and dry carefully with a clean tea-towel or kitchen roll.

2 Put the butter in a large, shallow oven-proof dish and heat in the oven until melted.

3 Add the potatoes and roll them around in the butter until they are coated.

4 Add the whole garlic cloves (peeled) and sprinkle the potatoes with salt and pepper.

5 Cover with tin foil and cook for 30 minutes.

6 Remove the foil, give the potatoes a little stir to cover them with more butter. Cook for another 20 minutes.

7 Grate the cheese and sprinkle over the top. Cook for 10 minutes or until the cheese bubbles.

8 Remove the garlic cloves before serving and sprinkle with the chives. Delicious!

Russia

The first course of a Russian dinner is called *zakuski*, meaning 'little bites'; these are starters or nibbles such as sausage slices, pickles, cheese and herrings (the wealthy would throw in extras like caviar and smoked salmon).

In the pre-Revolution years, Russian cuisine fell into two distinct parts. The aristocrats ate French food prepared by French chefs. Dishes of chicken and meat and out-of-season fruits and vegetables belonged in this half. The peasants, the vast bulk of the population, lived on black bread, porridge and soups. The most famous soup is *borshch*, made from beetroot and deep garnet red in colour – it is said that there are as many *borshch* recipes in Russia as there are grandmothers!

Here are two recipes from top tables, one named after the Romanoffs, the family that ruled Russia from 1613 to 1917, the other for *blinis* – easy to make and great finger food at parties.

Did you know? The very best caviar is dark-brown in colour, not black.

Romanoff Strawberries *
(serves 4)

---

1 large punnet fresh strawberries
$1/4$ cup orange juice (freshly squeezed if possible)
2 teaspoons finely grated orange peel
1 carton of whipped cream

Utensils: kitchen knife, chopping board, mixing bowl, metal spoon, serving dish

1 Wash the strawberries and cut each in half – *! watch fingers.*

2 Place the strawberries in a bowl with the orange juice and orange peel, and toss gently.

3 Top the strawberries with whipped cream and serve.

Smoked Salmon Blinis **
(makes 30)

1 cup self raising flour
2 eggs
$1/2$ cup milk
1 tablespoon sour cream
Topping:
$1/2$ cup sour cream
2 tablespoons mayonnaise
2 teaspoons lemon juice
1 tablespoon chives
1 tablespoon mint
6oz/175g smoked salmon

Utensils: mixing bowl, sieve, wooden spoon, frying pan, metal spoon, chopping board, kitchen knife, small bowl, fork

1 Sift the flour into a mixing bowl and make a well in the middle.

2   Beat the eggs in a small bowl with a fork and pour into the well. Add the milk and sour cream and stir until the batter is smooth. Leave the batter to stand for 10 minutes.

3   Chop the chives and mint into fine pieces on a chopping board with a kitchen knife – *! watch fingers*. Cut the salmon into thin slices.

4   Coat the bottom of the frying pan with oil and heat on a medium ring. Drop teaspoonfuls of the batter into the pan. When bubbles appear on the surface of the blinis turn them. Cook both sides until golden. Repeat until all the mixture has been used.

5   Place the sour cream, mayonnaise, lemon juice, chives and mint in a mixing bowl and mix together with a wooden spoon. Spoon some of the mixture on to each blini and top with a slice of smoked salmon.

Spain

A lot of Spanish cooking is influenced by North Africa or the East. The Moors from Africa ruled the south of Spain for hundreds of years; it was they who introduced the spices and exotic fruits of their fatherland. Later, in 1492, Christopher Columbus discovered America, bringing back not only gold but pepper, chillies, tomatoes and chocolate. Another world traveller, Vasco de Gama, sailed around Africa to India and he brought back more spices and new foods. No wonder Spanish cooking is so colourful and full of flavour.

Stews are very popular in Spain – they are called *cocidos*, which literally means 'boiled', because all the ingredients are boiled in water. They are a mixture of meat, chicken, sausages and vegetables, well flavoured with herbs and spices; the exact ingredients depend on where you are in Spain. In Castile it must contain chick-peas, potato, cabbage, meat, sowbelly and *chorizo*, the famous Spanish sausage. In Catalonia dumplings are obligatory. In Asturia, it's broad beans, pork sausages, black pudding, ham, bacon, pork, cooked with saffron and paprika. In Madrid the stew includes chick-peas, chicken and bacon, onions, leeks, tomatoes, potatoes, garlic sausage and carrots; as a garnish there are meatballs made from mince and breadcrumbs. The *cocido* is eaten in three stages – first the broth, then the vegetables, then the meat. Apart from being deliciously tasty, *cocidos* mean the whole meal is cooked in one pot. A great idea if you hate washing-up as much as I do!

Around the coast, *cocidos* are based on the fresh fish caught everywhere around the long coastline. My recipe, from the north coast, is a cod and vegetable stew. My other recipe is *paella*, that glorious colourful mix of seafood, chicken and peas, cooked with saffron-flavoured rice; I have used prawns but you can add lobster and mussels.

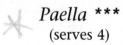

Paella ***
(serves 4)

---

1 large onion
1 red pepper
1 can tomatoes
2 cloves garlic
2 chicken fillets
1 chicken stock cube
3/4 pint/425ml boiling water
8oz/225g long-grained rice
5oz/150g prawns
2oz/50g frozen peas
2 tablespoons vegetable oil
1 tablespoon saffron
salt and pepper
1 lemon

Utensils: chopping board, kitchen knife, garlic crusher, frying pan with lid, wooden spoon, measuring jug

---

1   Chop the red pepper and the onion on a chopping board using a kitchen knife – *! watch fingers*.

2   Peel and crush the garlic cloves using a garlic crusher.

3   Cut the chicken into slices on a chopping board using a kitchen knife (you might find it easier and quicker to use a kitchen scissors instead) – *! watch fingers*.

4   Heat the oil in the frying pan and place the chicken in it carefully. Cook for 5–6 minutes until white.

5   Add the onion, salt and garlic to the pan and stir. Cook for a few more minutes until the onions are soft.

6   Open the tin of tomatoes and, using a kitchen knife, cut them into pieces while they are still in the tin. Add to the frying pan and stir again.

7   Dissolve the chicken stock cube in the boiling water in a heat-proof jug – *! watch steam*. Pour into the pan carefully.

8 Add the rice and saffron to the pan and stir gently. Place the lid on the pan and cook over a low heat for 20 minutes.

9 Add the frozen peas and the prawns to the pan and cook for another 5 minutes with the lid on.

10 Cut the lemon into wedges on a chopping board using a kitchen knife – *! watch fingers.* Arrange them on top of the paella and serve hot from the pan. As the Spanish say: *Buen apetito!*

Catalan Fish Stew **
(serves 4)

$1^1/_2$lb/675g cod pieces
1 medium onion
8oz/225g mushrooms
1 green pepper
1 heaped teaspoon brown sugar
8oz/225g tin of chopped tomatoes
4oz/110g butter
1 small packet of frozen peas
1 lemon
salt and pepper

Utensils: casserole dish, chopping board,
sharp knife, metal spoon

Preheat the oven to gas mark 4/175°C/350°F

---

1 Place the cod pieces in a buttered casserole dish. It's a good idea to ask an adult to prepare the fish

for you – all the bones need to be removed carefully.

2 Cut the lemon in half on the chopping board – *! watch fingers*. Squeeze the juice of half the lemon over the cod and season with salt and pepper.

3 Chop the onion into small pieces – *! watch fingers*. Wash and slice the mushrooms and pepper. Spread the vegetables, including the tinned tomatoes, over the cod.

4 Sprinkle the brown sugar over the top. Cut half the butter into pieces and place these on top too.

5 Cover the casserole dish with a buttered lid and bake in the oven for 30 minutes.

6 When the fish is cooked add the peas and the juice of the other lemon half. Return to the oven for 10 minutes until the peas are soft.

7 Serve immediately with potatoes or rice.

Scandinavia

There are five countries in this northern part of Europe – Sweden, Norway, Finland, Iceland and Denmark. Much of the area is forest, there are vast lakelands, and the long coastline means fishing is very important to the whole five.

Denmark is said to have as many pigs as people so pork is the national meat. It is usually served with apple sauce, meaning there are apple orchards, meaning apple pies of which the Danes are very fond. But probably Denmark is best known for its famous open sandwiches – *smorrebrod* (literally buttered bread), topped with such combinations as prawns and mushrooms, salami and tomatoes, cheese and anchovies, crisp-fried bacon and sausage, all held together with lettuce and mayonnaise. They are really substantial and eaten with a knife and fork.

In Norway, breakfast is the big meal of the day. If you're invited to one, expect to see a table groaning with fish of all kinds (herrings are the great favourite), cold meats, boiled eggs, and a delicious cheese called *gjetost* which tastes like fudge!

Sweden is home of the *smorgasbord,* that vast array of dishes laid out buffet-style from which everyone serves themselves. Herring, of course, *gravelax* (like our smoked salmon but cured with salt and spices rather than smoked). Change plates for the second course of meat, chicken, vegetables, with and without sauce, either warm or cold, with various salads. Change plates again for fruit and cheese.

Then have a rest!

Smorgasbord is a super party idea, especially if you encourage everyone to bring a plate of something.

The Scandinavians are dedicated fish eaters – that is why one of my recipes is for Tuna Pie, which is tasty and easy, perfect for a family supper. I serve it with a green salad and fresh crusty bread.

Smorrebrod *
(serves 4)

---

8 slices of brown bread
some butter
4 slices of red Cheddar cheese
a tin of anchovies
4 slices of salami
2 tomatoes
1 red onion

Utensils: chopping board, kitchen knife, serving plate, tin opener

---

1   Butter each slice of bread.

2   Using a kitchen knife – *! watch fingers* – cut the tomatoes and the onion into thin slices.

3   Place a slice of cheese on four of the slices of bread. Top two with tomato and two with anchovies in a criss-cross pattern.

4   Place the salami on the other four slices of bread. Top two with tomato and two with onion rings.

Scandinavian Tuna Pie *
(serves 4)

---

1 tin of tuna
1 medium onion
$1/2$ pint/275ml white sauce
6 medium potatoes
knob of butter
salt and pepper
a handful of fresh parsley, chopped
$1/4$ pint/150ml milk

Utensils: sharp knife, chopping board, frying pan, mixing bowl, fork, 2 saucepans, oven-proof dish, metal spoon, potato masher

---

Preheat oven to gas mark 5/190°C /375°F

---

1 Chop the onion into small pieces – *! watch fingers.* Place a knob of butter in the frying pan and fry the onion for about five minutes until soft.

2 Open the tuna can and drain the oil. Mash the tuna fish in a mixing bowl using a fork.

3 Peel and cut the potatoes into slices and boil until you can slip a knife easily through the pieces.

4 Make the white sauce either from a packet or your own (recipe on page 118).

5 Add the tuna and the onion to the white sauce mix and bring to the boil.

6 Mash the potatoes and add milk, a knob of butter, salt and pepper and the chopped parsley.

7 Place a layer of potato in the bottom of a buttered oven-proof dish. Then pour in the tuna and white sauce mix. Finish with a layer of potato.

8 Bake in the oven for 45 minutes. Serve piping hot with a green salad.

Danish Apple Strudel ******
(serves 4)

12oz/350g packet of frozen puff pastry
3 large green apples
$1/2$ cup sultanas
$1/4$ cup brown sugar
1 teaspoon grated lemon rind
$1/2$ teaspoon cinnamon
a little butter
a little plain flour

Utensils: rolling pin, mixing bowl, wooden spoon, metal spoon, chopping board, apple peeler, kitchen knife, small saucepan, pastry brush or teaspoon

Preheat the oven to gas mark 4/175°C/350°F

1   Thaw the pastry. Place on a clean, lightly floured counter or table-top and roll out into a rectangle about 10 inches by 14 inches.

2   Peel and core the apples and slice thinly – *! watch fingers*. Place in a mixing bowl. Stir in the sultanas, brown sugar, lemon rind and cinnamon and mix together.

3   Spread the filling on to the pastry, leaving an inch of bare pastry around the sides.

4   Roll the pastry up and seal the edges, pressing firmly. The pastry should look like a thick sausage roll.

5   Melt some butter in a small saucepan.

6   Place the strudel on a greased baking tray and brush with the melted butter (use a pastry brush or spoon over with a teaspoon). Bake for 15–20 minutes until the pastry is golden brown.

7   Serve with custard or cream.

Switzerland

Swiss cooking is very varied. Not surprising when you realise that Switzerland is really three countries, all with their own languages, customs and cuisines. The biggest part is German-Switzerland. French-Switzerland borders Lake Geneva, and the Italian-speaking part is beside Lake Lugano. So the cooking can be either German, French or Italian.

Traditional in German-Switzerland are two great potato recipes: *rosti*, an onion-flavoured potato cake, and *raclette*, which you could describe as a type of cheesy potatoes. It is mentioned in the famous Swiss book *Heidi* by Johanna Spyri. Heidi is a little girl who lives in the Alps with her grandfather. When she is eight her aunt takes her away to live in the city. But don't worry – there's a happy ending!

Delicious on a cold winter night, *raclettes* are easy to cook and make a great snack.

Raclette *
(serves 4)

---

4 medium potatoes
8oz/225g Swiss cheese – Gruyere or Emmenthal
a little butter
salt and pepper

---

1 Scrub the potatoes carefully and place in a saucepan of cold water (don't peel them).

2   Bring to the boil and simmer until cooked (about 15 minutes). You can tell they're done by sticking a knife into them – if it goes in easily they're ready.

3   Take them carefully out of the water and cut each in half – *! watch fingers*.

4   Put a pinch of salt and pepper and a small blob of butter on each. Top with a generous slice of cheese.

5   Put the potatoes halves under the grill until the cheese bubbles gently.

Israel

Jewish people live all over the world, from Israel to Ireland to New York. Everywhere they have brought their own cooking and their various festivals. From them Spain inherited the *cocido* or stew. The Jewish version, based on eggs, was left simmering all through Friday nights for eating on Saturday when no cooking was allowed. In the terrible days of the Spanish Inquisition, the Jews, in order to prove to their neighbours that they had renounced their Jewish faith and become Christians, had to substitute pork for eggs. This was a terrible decision to have to make as the Jews were forbidden to eat pork,

Every year in the Jewish month of Kislev (December) the festival of *Hanukkah* is celebrated. Symbolising the miracle at the temple of Jerusalem over 2000 years ago, it is called 'The Festival of Lights' and a traditional candlestick which holds ornamental candles, called a *hanukkiya*, is lit; every night of the festival a new candle is added. Like Christmas, *Hanukkah* is a time of family celebration and many Jewish people give and receive gifts and have family meals together. Special dishes include *latkes* (potato cakes), served with apple sauce and sour cream, and a plaited bread called *challah*.

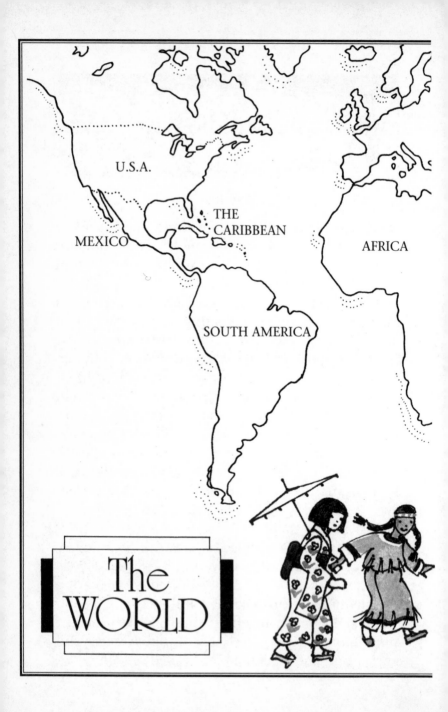

U.S.A.

MEXICO

THE
CARIBBEAN

SOUTH AMERICA

AFRICA

The
WORLD

Purim is another Jewish festival held in February or March to celebrate Queen Esther who saved the Jews from the evil Haman, the king's adviser. At *Purim,* small triangular pastries called *hamantashen* are eaten; they represent Haman's ears!

Latkes **
(serves 4)

---

4 medium potatoes
1 medium onion
1 egg
salt and pepper
3 tablespoons vegetable oil

Utensils: potato peeler, grater, sharp knife,
2 mixing bowls, sieve, frying pan, wooden spoon,
tablespoon, metal spatula, kitchen roll,
serving plate

---

1 Peel the potatoes and grate – *! watch fingers*. Place in a mixing bowl and cover with cold water to prevent the potatoes from browning.

2 Peel away the outer layer of the onion and grate – *! watch fingers*. Mix in a bowl with the egg and a pinch of salt and pepper.

3 Place the grated potato in a sieve and drain off the water. Add to the egg mixture and stir with the wooden spoon.

4 Heat the oil in the frying pan. Put tablespoons of the mixture into the pan and press flat.

5 Fry each *latke* for 5–6 minutes on each side. When cooled, place them on a sheet of kitchen paper on a plate and serve immediately.

Mandarin Cheesecake *
(makes 1)

According to legend, cheesecake reminds the Jews of the prophet Moses. He waited so long for God to give him the Ten Commandments that the milk had turned to cheese!

4oz/110g digestive biscuits
2oz/50g butter
8oz/225g cream cheese
8oz/225g tin of mandarins
1 packet of lemon jelly
3/4 pint/425ml cream

Utensils: measuring jug, 2 mixing bowls, large saucepan, wooden spoon, cheesecake dish, electric or hand-held whip

---

1 Drain the mandarin oranges and keep the juice. The easiest way is to open the tin, leave the lid in place and use the lid to strain off the juice into a bowl.

2 Melt the lemon jelly in 1/4 pint boiling water and add 1/4 pint of the mandarin juice. Leave to cool.

3 Crush the digestives in a large mixing bowl with your fingers and a wooden spoon.

4 Melt the butter in a large saucepan and put in the crushed biscuits. Mix together with the wooden spoon.

5 Spoon the biscuit mixture into the bottom of the cheesecake dish and leave aside.

6 Cream the cheese in a mixing bowl. Put some mandarin pieces aside for decoration later. Chop the mandarins and add to the cheese. Mix gently, trying not to crush the mandarins.

7 Add the jelly to the cheese and mandarin mixture.

8 Whip the cream and carefully fold into the cheese and jelly mix.

9 Pour the mixture on to the biscuit base and set in the fridge for 3–4 hours.

10 Decorate the top with whole mandarin pieces.

You could also make raspberry cheesecake by replacing the mandarins with 1 punnet fresh raspberries (or an 8oz/225g tin) and using raspberry jelly instead of lemon jelly.

Iran, Iraq, Saudi Arabia

Iran, Iraq and Saudi Arabia are three of the twenty separate countries that make up the Middle East. Much of the land is desert but in the fertile parts the farmers keep sheep and goats and grow fruit and vegetables such as melons, cucumber, lemons, chickpeas and brown beans. Rice is popular, so are kebabs, and everywhere they make delicious sweets and pastries. In the *souks* (indoor markets) you can buy every kind of spice.

Did you know? It's traditional for Eastern families to remain silent while eating. Could you do that?

Hummus *
(serves 4 to 6)

Hummus is a tasty starter or dip made from chickpeas. In the Middle East starters are called *mezze*.

---

1 lb/450g tin chick-peas
3 tablespoons lemon juice
2 tablespoons olive oil
2 cloves garlic
salt and pepper
1 tablespoon *tahini* (sesame seed) paste,
– optional

Utensils: electric blender, chopping board, sharp knife, metal spoon

---

1   Peel and crush the garlic on the chopping board.

2 Add all the ingredients to the blender and 'whoosh' for 30 seconds until smooth.

3 Serve with warmed pitta bread or toast.

Tabbouleh or Tabouli *
(serves 4 to 6)

A traditional recipe using *burghul* or cracked wheat – a delicious summer dish. There is a lot of chopping involved so adult help might be a good idea.

1/4 cup of *burghul* (cracked wheat)
2 medium tomatoes
1 medium onion
1/2 cup parsley
1/4 cup fresh mint
1/2 cup coriander
1 cup lemon juice

Utensils: mixing bowl, fork, chopping bowl, kitchen knife, metal spoon

1 Place the *burghul* in a bowl and cover with warm water. Leave to soak for 10 minutes. Spread on a clean tea-towel to dry.

2 Cut the tomatoes in half. Remove and discard seeds and pulp. Cut into small pieces on a chopping board with a sharp knife – *! watch fingers*.

3 Remove the skin and cut the onion into small pieces – *! watch fingers*.

4 Chop parsley, mint and coriander – *! watch fingers*.

5 Place all the ingredients in the mixing bowl and mix gently with a fork. Add the lemon juice and mix again.

The Far East

Honest now – you haven't a clue about Asia! Where it begins or ends.

The solution is simple; just look at the maps on pages 76 and 77. East from Iran lie India, China and Japan. South of China you'll find Vietnam, Indonesia and, if you go far enough, you'll come to another continent – Australia and New Zealand.

India

The old 'India' is now three countries – India, Pakistan and Bangladesh. In all three, spices are a vital part of their cooking; indeed the word 'curry' comes from the Indian *kahri*, meaning spice sauce. Over a hundred exist and you're probably familiar with some of them – pepper, ginger, tumeric, coriander, cumin, fenugreek, fennel, saffron, cardamon, cinnamon, cloves, sesame, mustard seed, mace, chilli. Whether your curry is mild, hot or very hot depends on the particular mix you use.

There is no one standard mix; chefs and restaurants everywhere have their own jealously guarded recipes. Why not try out various combinations and find out which you like best?

Curries and other spiced dishes are always served

with rice and various accompaniments such as chutneys or pickles, yoghurt salads and flat breads like naan, chapates and poppadums. Coconut milk is used in many recipes.

Did you know? The traditional way of eating in India is with the right hand. Hindus eat no meat because they believe the cow is sacred.

Tandoori Chicken ***
(serves 4)

Tandoori derives from the earthenware oven Indians use but an ordinary oven will do just as well. This recipe needs some traditional Indian ingredients – ginger, *garam masala* and chilli powder – which can be bought in most large supermarkets. It requires lots of preparation, but you'll be really pleased with the result.

---

4 chicken fillets
1 inch chopped ginger
2 tablespoons vinegar
3 teaspoons *garam masala*
2 cloves of garlic
juice of 1 lemon
$1/2$ teaspoon chilli powder
salt

Utensils: sharp knife, chopping board, mixing bowl, metal spoon, baking dish

---

Preheat the oven to gas mark 4/175°C/350°F

---

1   With a sharp knife make slices in the chicken fillets, making sure not to cut the whole way through – *! watch fingers*.

2   Place the fillets in a dish. Rub the salt and lemon juice into the fillets with your fingers. Put aside for half an hour.

3   Place the ginger, vinegar, garlic and chilli powder in a bowl and mix together. Pour over the chicken and leave overnight in the fridge. This makes the chicken very tasty.

4   Bake for 60 minutes. Sprinkle with *garam masala* (a powder made of spices). Serve with rice.

Lassi *
(makes 2)

Lassi is a traditional Indian drink made with yoghurt. It is very refreshing, ideal for drinking with curry. It has an unusual flavour – try it and see!

---

1 cup ice water
$1/2$ cup plain yogurt (unflavoured)
$1/2$ teaspoon salt
$1/2$ teaspoon ground cumin

Utensils: a jar with a screw-top lid, teaspoon, cup

---

1   Place all the ingredients in a tightly closed jar and shake until mixed together.

2   Serve with curry or just on its own.

China

The Chinese had a civilisation stretching back for hundreds of years while most of Europe was living in mud huts. So they've had time to develop their cooking into a fine art. And eating is important to the Chinese; instead of saying, 'Hello, how are you?' they say, 'Have you eaten?'

In Canton, one of the provinces of the country, they love sweet-and-sour combinations, using fruit like pineapple, tangerines and lemons with meat of all kinds (always with soy sauce); it is also famous for its *dim sum* – small pastries filled with pork, beef or seafood. In Szechuan (where the pandas live) they love spicy – and often very hot – dishes; many recipes use bamboo shoots which are, of course, the pandas' favourite food. Bejing (once called Peking) is best known for Peking duck – served in a pancake.

The writer Charles Lamb tells of how the Chinese discovered roast pork. According to this story, as a servant was cooking pork one day the house went on fire. When the flames were put out, the family thought the dinner had been ruined; instead they discovered delicious roast pork. So everyone started to burn their houses down – to produce this rare delicacy. Eventually they found it tasted just as good when they used an oven!

The Chinese love exotic foods. One of their favourites is thousand-year-eggs – uncooked eggs are covered with clay and buried in the ground for weeks (not years).

Did you know? Chopsticks are used for eating. They can be made of bamboo, wood, plastic, silver or gold.

Canton Sweet and Sour Pork Chops **
(serves 4)

---

4 pork chops
3 rings of pineapple (tinned)
3 tablespoons tomato purée
1 tablespoon soy sauce
1 tablespoon Worcester sauce
3 tablespoons cider vinegar
3 tablespoons pineapple juice (from tin)
1 green pepper
1 red pepper
$1^1/_2$ tablespoons honey
$1^1/_2$ tablespoons cornflour
4 tablespoons chicken stock (stock cube)
Rice:
long grain or basmati rice for 4

Utensils: Chopping board, sharp knife, mixing bowl, wooden spoon, casserole dish, frying pan, spatula

---

Preheat oven to gas mark 4/175°C/350°F

---

1   Place the chops in a frying pan with a little oil and fry until brown.

2   Chop the pineapple rings into chunky pieces. Cut the peppers in half, remove the seeds and pulp and cut into thin slices – *! watch fingers.*

3 Place the chops, pineapple chunks and peppers in a casserole dish.

4 Mix together the tomato purée, soy sauce, Worcester sauce, vinegar, pineapple juice and honey in a bowl.

5 Stir the chicken stock into the cornflour in a small bowl and add this to the other sauce ingredients.

6 Pour the sauce over the chops and cover the casserole dish with its lid. Cook in the oven for 60 minutes.

7 Cook the rice, following the instructions on the packet.

8 Serve the chops with the rice.

Japan

If you were invited to a traditional Japanese meal, you would sit on the ground at a table about a foot high. Before you would be set various dishes such as rice, cod, tuna, mackerel, perhaps lobster and shrimp, seasoned with soybean sauce. Afterwards there would be fresh fruit – plums, apricots, cherries, apples and pears. To drink: green tea.

Japan is made up to four islands. The land is very mountainous, making farming difficult. Its people like plain food, simply prepared, with the emphasis on fish, fruit and vegetables, though western-style food, even hamburgers, is now eaten almost everywhere. Meat was once forbidden by the Buddhist religion and only permitted in the mid-1900s. Fish is still the most popular choice, though if you're offered *toto fuga* (tiger fish) which is eaten raw, think twice; unless it has been properly prepared, it will poison you! *Sushi* (raw fish Japanese style), now available in Ireland, is perfectly safe.

Did you know? Rice is such an important crop that the word for it – gohan – also means food.

Parent and Child Rice Bowl **
(serves 4)

I love the descriptive name of this recipe. Chicken and egg – parent and child. The Japanese spoon the eggs over the hot rice when they are still quite runny and allow the heat to cook them. It's a simple but very tasty dish, and I hope you enjoy it.

1 chicken fillet
1 cup short-grained rice
$1/2$ teaspoon salt
2 $1/2$ cups chicken stock (stock cube)
$1/3$ cup soy sauce (*tamari*)
2 tablespoons sugar
3 scallions
4 large eggs
2 cups water

Utensils: large saucepan, wooden spoon, large frying pan, chopping board, kitchen knife, cup, fork

1 Place the water in a saucepan and add the rice and salt. Bring to the boil and simmer for 20 minutes, until the rice is tender. (Rice varies according to variety and brand, so check the packet for details of cooking times).

2 Chop the chicken into thin strips on a chopping board, using a knife. I find it easier to snip chicken with a kitchen scissors, so use these if you can – *! watch fingers.*

3 Chop the scallions into thin pieces on a chopping board using a knife – *! watch fingers.*

4 Place the chicken stock, soy sauce and sugar in the pan and bring the mixture to the boil, stirring with a wooden spoon.

5 Add the scallions and the chicken and cook for 5–6 minutes.

6 Break the eggs into a bowl and beat lightly using a fork. Add to the pan and stir with a fork until they have cooked, about 3–4 minutes.

7 Place the cooked rice in soup bowls and spoon some egg and chicken mixture over the top.

Ginger Pork Chops **
(serves 4)

---

2 tablespoons soy sauce (*tamari*)
1 tablespoon grated fresh ginger
(you can buy fresh ginger from most large supermarkets)
2 cloves garlic, crushed
4 boneless pork loin chops (about 4oz each)

Utensils: mixing bowl, wooden spoon, garlic crusher, grater

---

1 Place the soy sauce, ginger and crushed garlic in a mixing bowl and stir.

2 Place the pork chops in the bowl, one by one, until they are well coated with the mixture on both sides.

3 Put the chops on a plate and cover with cling film. Leave to stand for 20 minutes.

4 Preheat the grill. Place the chops on the grill and cook each side for 5–6 minutes, until tender.

5 Serve with boiled rice.

Vietnam

South of China, east of Thailand, Vietnam is really four countries – North Vietnam, South Vietnam, Cambodia and Laos. Many different nations have ruled over parts of it, including the Chinese and the French (who called their colony Indo-China). So it never really had a chance to develop a distinctive cuisine of its own. Cooking is heavily influenced by Chinese, Thai and French food (even today you can get excellent French bread and rolls from the French bakeries that exist in many of the cities).

Rice is eaten every single day. And for breakfast you might be offered a choice of porridge or noodle soup. *Chuc qui'ban thanh cong!* as they say in Vietnam; it means 'Happy cooking!'

The north part of the country grows great crops of oranges, tangerines, pineapples and bananas. Try the latter the Hanoi way.

Hanoi Bananas **
(serves 4)

---

2 medium bananas
2 tablespoons butter
2 tablespoons brown sugar
8 scoops banana or vanilla ice-cream

Utensils: frying pan, spatula, metal spoon,
tablespoon, chopping board, knife

1　Peel the bananas and slice into $1/2$ inch slices on a chopping board – *! watch fingers*.

2　Melt the butter in the frying pan over a medium heat and add the brown sugar. Stir until smooth.

3　Add the banana slices in a single layer and cook for 2–3 minutes until lightly brown. Turn once.

4　Place the ice-cream in glass dishes and top with the warm bananas. Yum!

Indonesia

What's in a name? Indonesia was once the Dutch East Indies. Since independence in 1945 its official name is Indonesia, though some people still call it the Spice Islands. It's really a collection of over 300 small islands, stretching along the Equator from the China Sea to the Indian Ocean and includes Bali, Java, Sumatra, the Celebes, and the former Borneo. More coconuts are grown here than anywhere else in the world and many recipes use coconut milk and coconut flesh.

It's the home of *rijstaffel* (rice table) which the Dutch brought home with them to the Netherlands. Another of their dishes is Beef Satay, pieces of grilled beef (*sate*) which are dipped into bowls of peanut sauce. And as you've probably guessed, it's spices with everything – ginger, coriander, tumeric, pepper, lemon grass, cloves...

Beef Satay with Peanut Sauce **
(serves 4)

---

1 lb/450g Irish sirloin beef
Marinade:
2 tablespoons soy sauce
1 tablespoon brown sugar
1 tablespoon vegetable oil
1 garlic clove
Sauce:
1/4 cup hot water
1/4 cup creamy peanut butter
1 tablespoon lime or lemon juice
1 teaspoon brown sugar

Utensils: 8 wooden skewers, chopping board, sharp
knife, 2 mixing bowls, metal spoon, cling film,
pastry brush

---

1 Cut the beef into thin strips on a chopping board using a sharp knife – *! watch fingers.*

2 Put the soy sauce, sugar and vegetable oil into a bowl.

3 Crush the garlic on a chopping board and add to the bowl. Mix the ingredients together.

4 Place the beef in the bowl and make sure each piece is covered in marinade. Cover with cling film and leave aside for 30 minutes.

5 Place the hot water and peanut butter in the second bowl and mix until smooth. Add the lime juice and sugar and mix well.

6 Lift the beef strips out of the marinade using a metal spoon. Thread them on to the skewers carefully, making 's' shapes with the meat.

7 Grill each skewer for 8–10 minutes until cooked. Brush the skewers with the remaining marinade while they cook.

8 Serve the skewers with the peanut sauce.

Coconut Chicken **
(serves 4)

---

4 chicken breasts
3 tablespoons vegetable oil
2 onions
2 cloves garlic
2oz/50g cream of coconut
$1/2$ pint/275ml hot water

1 tablespoon lemon juice
1 tablespoon ground ginger
1 tablespoon chilli powder
salt and pepper

Utensils: large frying pan, wooden spoon, kitchen roll, bowl, metal spoon, garlic crusher, chopping board, sharp knife

---

1   Place the oil in the frying pan and heat gently. Place the chicken breasts in the pan and cook for about 5 minutes on each side.

2   Chop the onions into small pieces on a chopping board using a sharp kitchen knife – *! watch fingers*. Peel and crush the garlic using a garlic crusher.

3   Place the cooked chicken pieces on some kitchen roll and sprinkle them with the chilli powder, ginger and lemon juice.

4   Place the onions and garlic in the frying pan and cook for a few minutes until the onions are soft.

5   Place the coconut cream in a bowl and add the hot water. Stir until it has dissolved and you are left with a white, milky liquid.

6   Put the chicken back in the pan with the onions and garlic. Carefully pour the coconut milk over the chicken. Cook over a low heat for 30–40 minutes.

7   Serve with boiled rice.

Africa

Africa is the world's largest continent: it's also the hottest. There are over fifty independent countries, from Algeria and Zambia, and it is home to over six hundred million people. Cooking depends on the crops grown and the legacy of conquerors and settlers, from the *cous-cous* (made from semolina) and lamb stews of the north coast, to the Dutch dishes and Malayan stews of South Africa.

Much of African food is hot and spicy. A pepper called *pilli-pilli* is used to flavour stews and an old African tradition holds that a husband can tell how much a wife loves him by the amount of pepper she uses; if she uses a lot, it means she really loves him!

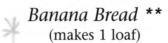

Banana Bread **
(makes 1 loaf)

8oz/225g sugar
1 lb/450g plain flour
3 ripe bananas
4oz/110g butter
2 teaspoons baking powder
4oz/110g chopped nuts (optional)
3 eggs

Utensils: large baking tin, mixing bowl, wooden spoon, sieve, fork, small bowl

---

Preheat the oven to gas mark 4/175°C/350°F

---

1 Place the butter and sugar in a mixing bowl and cream together.

2 Beat the eggs in a small bowl using a fork. Beat into the butter and sugar mixture.

3 Sift the flour and baking powder. Mash the bananas in a small bowl using a fork.

4 Add a little flour to the mixture and then a little banana. Continue adding flour and banana, mixing well as you go along. Stir in the nuts.

5 Place in a greased baking tin and bake for 1 hour.

6 Cool on a wire rack.

Kenyan Crunchy Bananas **
(serves 2)

---

1 tablespoon butter
1 tablespoon brown sugar
$1/4$ teaspoon cinnamon
2 large bananas
$1/4$ cup chopped unsalted peanuts

Utensils: saucepan, wooden spoon, baking pan (or tray with sides), chopping board, kitchen knife, pastry brush, metal spoon

---

Preheat the oven to gas mark 5/190°C/ 375°F

---

1   Place the butter in a saucepan and melt over a low heat. Stir in the sugar and cinnamon until mixed well together.

2   Grease the baking pan. Peel the bananas and cut each in half on a chopping board using a kitchen knife – *! watch fingers.*

3   Place each banana half, with the flat cut side facing down, in the pan. Brush each with some of the sugar mixture and sprinkle with the chopped peanuts. If you don't have a brush, spoon it on instead.

4   Bake for 20 minutes until the bananas are light brown.

5   Serve warm, topped with whipped cream. Delicious!

Australia is both a country and a continent, home to the wombat, the kangaroo, the dingo and the koala bear. The native people of Australia are the Aborigines; the original inhabitants of New Zealand are the Maoiri.

Australia and New Zealand are both great meat-producing countries – Australia for beef, New Zealand for lamb – and people prefer it simply prepared. No frills! Outdoor cooking or barbecuing is very popular in both countries, especially in Australia because of the hot climate. At Christmas, our midsummer, Australians eat turkey, mince pies and plum pudding – on the beach!

Cookery in both countries developed from the European and Asian recipes brought over by the early settlers. About the only original contribution they made was 'damper' or bushman's bread, a squashed ball of flour and water dough, cooked in the hot ashes of the fire. However, some people claim that the delicious meringue dessert – the Pavlova – had its origins down under. Anna Pavlova, probably the best known Russian ballerina, took her ballet company all over the world. She visited New Zealand in 1926 and the Pavlova, which resembles a tutu, was said to have been invented in her honour.

Barbecue Chicken Drumsticks **
(serves 12)

---

12 chicken drumsticks
Sauce:
2 tablespoons honey
1 tablespoon Worcester sauce
juice of 1/2 orange
grated rind of 1/2 orange
1 tablespoon tomato purée
1 tablespoon soy sauce

Utensils: mixing bowl, metal spoon, pastry brush,
tin foil

---

1   Place all the sauce ingredients in a bowl and mix
together.

2   Brush the sauce over the drumsticks with a pastry
brush. Leave a little sauce in the bowl to baste the
drumsticks while cooking.

3   Place the drumsticks on a large piece of tin foil
and fold over to cover them. Leave aside for 1
hour.

4   Remove the tin foil and place the drumsticks on
the barbecue grid to cook for 20 minutes, turning
now and again. While they are cooking, spoon
the rest of the sauce over the drumsticks.

5   Serve hot with salads and baked potatoes.

New Zealand Lamb Hot Pot **
(serves 4)

---

1 lb/450g lamb, cubed
1 lb/450g carrots
2 onions
2 tablespoons vegetable oil
1 teaspoon grated nutmeg
1 tablespoon tomato purée
3/4 pint/425ml lamb stock
1 tablespoon Worcester sauce
4oz/110g red split lentils
salt and pepper

Utensils: oven-proof casserole dish, wooden spoon, chopping board

---

Preheat the oven to gas mark 5/190°C/375°F

---

1   Slice the carrots and onions thinly on a chopping board – ! *watch fingers.*

2   Heat the oil in the oven-proof casserole dish and cook the cubed lamb until brown.

3   Add the onion and the carrots. Cook for about 10 minutes, until the vegetables begin to brown.

4   Add the nutmeg, tomato purée, Worcester sauce and lamb stock and bring the mixture to the boil.

5   Wash the lentils in cold water and add them to the mixture.

6   Put the lid on and cook for 60 minutes.

7   Serve with potatoes and green vegetables.

Strawberry Pavlova *
(serves 8)

---

1 meringue case
1/2 pint/275ml whipping cream
12 oz/350g strawberries (2 punnets)
1 tablespoon caster sugar

Utensils: mixing bowl, electric whisk, chopping
board, kitchen knife, colander, metal spoon

---

1   Whip the cream and the sugar in a mixing bowl
using an electric whisk.

2   Spoon the cream into the meringue shell.

3   Wash the strawberries and remove the husks (the
leaves and green bits). Halve each strawberry on
the chopping board with a kitchen knife.

4   Place the strawberries on the cream and serve
immediately. Pure Pavlova delight!

U.S.A.

In 1621 the first settlers arrived in America from England and endured a winter of terrible cold and starvation. The following harvest was good and they thanked God for the crops by holding a great feast to praise Him. Now every year, on the fourth Thursday of November, families all over North America celebrate Thanksgiving Day in memory of those settlers. The whole family reunites for the day, often travelling from other states or countries. They eat turkey, sweet potatoes, pumpkin and cranberry sauce, all foods that would have been eaten at that first Thanksgiving. Afterwards there are delicious pies, filled with apple, pecan nuts or pumpkin.

But the vast continent that is North America isn't only about turkey. Each region has its own special way of cooking. The north-east is fish soup country, especially clam chowder, and other specialities include shoofly pie, Boston baked beans and chicken a la king. The south-east offers Creole cooking; sweet potato pie, black bean soup, southern fried chicken, chicken Maryland, oysters Rockefeller and hush-puppies (cornmeal cakes – pieces of which were thrown to the dogs to keep them quiet). Down Texas way, we're in Tex-Mex country and dishes from Texas and Mexico blend in seamlessly – *chilli con carne* (a meat stew), *tortillas* (flat cornmeal bread), which become *enchiladas* when they're stuffed, *frijoles* (Mexican beans) and other spicy dishes.

Steak? James Beard's *American Cookery* lists forty-five recipes for various kinds of steak, from 'carpetbagger' (with oysters), to 'sons of rest' (with butter and mustard), to 'porterhouse' (named for the porterhouses on coach stops in olden days.

Every American kitchen has its cookie jar, named after the Dutch *kockjes,* and the variety of cakes is legion, including the marvellously named 1-2-3-4 cake (l cup of butter, 2 of sugar, 3 of flour and 4 eggs). And, of course, the national dish is the hamburger.

Did you know? The famous Caesar Salad (iceberg lettuce, diced bread, olive oil, garlic, cloves, anchovy fillets, eggs and Parmesan cheese) is not American at all; it was created in Mexico in the 1920s.

Chocolate Chip Cakes **
(makes 16)

4oz/110g soft butter
4oz/110g caster sugar
2 eggs
4oz/110g self raising flour, sifted
2oz/50g chocolate chips or chopped plain chocolate

Utensils: large mixing bowl, wooden spoon, metal spoon, 16 paper cases, 2 baking trays, dessert spoon

---

Preheat oven to gas mark 5/190°C/375°F

---

1 Cream the butter and the sugar together in a large mixing bowl using a wooden spoon.

2 Beat in the eggs whole, one at a time. Gently fold in the flour using a metal spoon. Stir in the chocolate chips or the plain chocolate chopped very fine.

3 Place a dessertspoon of mixture into each of the paper bun cases. Place the bun cases on baking trays. Bake in the oven for 20–25 minutes until golden.

4 Cool the buns on a wire rack.

American Hamburgers **
(serves 4)

---

1 lb/450g Irish minced beef
1 egg
1 medium onion, chopped finely
1 tablespoon of vegetable oil
4 hamburger baps
2 tomatoes, sliced
1/4 iceberg lettuce, shredded
2 tablespoons mayonnaise
4oz/110g grated Cheddar cheese (optional)
salt and pepper
a handful of flour

Utensils: 2 mixing bowls (1 small and 1 large), wooden spoon, chopping board, frying pan, spatula

1   Beat the egg with a fork in a small mixing bowl.

2   Place the beef, onion, beaten egg and a pinch of salt and pepper in a large mixing bowl. Mix together with a wooden spoon. Using clean hands, squeeze the meat into 4 large balls. Place each ball on to a counter or table-top and pat into a burger shape, about 1/2 inch thick. You may need to sprinkle some flour on the counter to prevent the mixture from sticking.

3   Place the oil in a frying pan on a medium heat. Place the burgers in the pan and fry for about 6 minutes on both sides until dark brown.

4   When the burgers are cooked place each on a bap. Top with some shredded lettuce, some slices of tomato and a large dollop of mayonnaise. Sprinkle the grated cheese over the top.

5   Serve immediately.

You could add tomato sauce and mustard for extra taste.

American Hot Chicken Salad **

(serves 4)

12oz/350g cooked chicken
4 spring onions finely sliced
1/2 pt/275ml mayonnaise
2 teaspoons lemon juice
4oz/110g mature Cheddar cheese, grated
salt and pepper
a crushed packet of crisps (optional)

Utensils: chopping board, teaspoon, shallow, oven-proof dish, cheese grater, bowl, metal spoon

---

Preheat oven to gas mark 7/220°C/425°F

---

1 Put the chicken, spring onions, lemon juice and mayonnaise into a bowl with about three-quarters of the cheese.

2 Add a pinch of salt and pepper. Stir together and place in a shallow oven-proof dish.

3 Top with the rest of the cheese and the crushed crisps. Cook for 12–15 minutes. Be careful not to cook for any longer than this or the sauce will separate and go funny.

Serve with a green salad and crusty bread.

To crush the crisps – leave them in the closed bag, open it a little to let some air in and mash carefully in your hands.

Mexico
South America

Both Mexico and the continent of South America have much in common when it comes to cooking. Spanish influence is strong, though with regional differences. Everywhere lots of fruit and vegetables; in Peru they had over a hundred varieties of potato about the year 2500BC, and they also discovered a way to preserve vegetables by freeze-drying them!

In the Argentine steak is as popular as it is in the States but in the poorer countries, meat is used sparingly, usually as fillings for *tacos* – maize pancakes which are baked into crisp curved shapes.

Chicken Tacos **
(makes 2)

2 chicken breasts
oil for frying
1 tomato, sliced
1 small onion, finely chopped
juice of $1/2$ a lemon
a handful of shredded lettuce
a handful of grated red or white Cheddar
1 tablespoon mayonnaise
2 tablespoons guacamole or sour cream (optional)
2 taco shells

Utensils: frying pan, spatula, chopping board, sharp knife, metal spoon, mixing bowl

---

1 Gently cook the chicken in oil in the frying pan until brown – 10–15 minutes.

2 Chop the cooked chicken into small pieces. Place in a bowl. Add a pinch of salt and pepper, the lemon juice and onion. Stir gently.

3 Place half the chicken mixture into each taco shell.

4 Add lettuce, tomato and some grated cheese. Spoon a dollop of sour cream or guacamole over the top and serve immediately.

You could also try mince tacos – 1/2 lb minced beef, 1 chopped onion, salt and pepper.

Guacamole *
(serves 6)

Guacamole is a delicious dip made with mashed avocadoes. Serve it with Pringles, crisps or tortilla chips.

---

3 ripe avocadoes
1 tablespoon olive oil
1 tablespoon mayonnaise
salt and pepper
1 tablespoon lemon juice
1 ripe tomato chopped finely

Utensils: chopping board, sharp knife, mixing bowl, fork, metal spoon, serving bowl

---

1   Halve the avocadoes on a chopping board and remove the stones – *! watch fingers.* Scoop out the flesh and place in a mixing bowl.

2   Mash with a fork. Add the other ingredients and mix together until quite smooth.

3   Place in a bowl and serve immediately.

Be warned – guacamole goes brown if left in the air too long. Cover with cling film to keep it green!

Extra-Special Guacamole **
(serves 6)

This is the guacamole I serve at parties because it's extra delicious! Make as ordinary guacamole but add the extra ingredients at step 2.

---

2 ripe avocadoes
2 tablespoons sour cream
1 tablespoon mayonnaise
4 tablespoons lemon juice
1 teaspoon cumin
1 teaspoon coriander
1 clove crushed garlic
1 finely chopped tomato
1 tablespoon chopped chives or
1 small chopped onion
salt and pepper
2 or 3 drops of Tabasco sauce

The Caribbean

There are over one hundred islands in the Caribbean, stretching over 25,000 miles from Florida to South America. They became known as the West Indies and they are just as beautiful and interesting today as they were back in 1492 when Christopher Columbus described them as 'paradise'.

The islands were invaded at different times by Spain, Portugal, the Netherlands, France and Britain, all bringing their own eating habits with them, and these influences, as well as the wealth of raw materials available, came together to produce what we now know as Caribbean food. Wheat had to be imported so the native cooks supplemented it with *cassava*, a root which produces a flour-like substance.

Unusual Caribbean fruits include 'soursops' which have bumpy green skin and soft white flesh, 'star apples' whose pips form a star shape in the middle, 'naseberries' and 'paw-paws'.

Try these recipes and taste the Caribbean sun!

Caribbean Dip *
(serves 4)

8oz/225g cream cheese
4 tablespoons natural yoghurt
3oz/75g ham, cubed
6 tablespoons crushed pineapple, drained
salt and pepper
2 carrots
1 cucumber
celery
1 red pepper
1 yellow pepper

Utensils: mixing bowl, wooden spoon, sharp knife, cutting board, serving dish, plate

---

1   Place the cream cheese in a bowl and stir with the wooden spoon to soften.

2   Add the yoghurt gradually, stirring all the time.

3   Add the ham, pineapple and a pinch of salt and pepper.

4   Wash each vegetable and using a sharp knife cut into strips – *! watch fingers.*

5   Place the dip in a serving dish and arrange the vegetables on a plate.

Fruit Smoothies *
(serves 2)

---

2 cups of fresh strawberries or frozen strawberries
(if using fresh strawberries add 3 or 4 ice-cubes)
1 ripe banana
$1/2$ cup pineapple juice

Utensils: blender or food processor, knife,
chopping board, 2 glasses

---

1 Cut the banana into chunks using a knife –
! watch fingers.

2 Place the strawberries, banana and juice in a
blender or food processor and 'whoosh' until
smooth.

3 Pour into two glasses and serve.

Pineapple Bread **
(makes 1 loaf)

4oz/110g butter
6oz/175g brown sugar
1 small can of crushed pineapple
12oz/350g mixed fruit
8oz/225g self raising flour
2 eggs

Utensils: saucepan, wooden spoon, mixing bowl,
fork, 2 lb loaf tin

Preheat the oven to gas mark 3/165°C/325°F

1 Mix together in a saucepan the butter, sugar, pineapple and mixed fruit.

2 Bring the mixture to the boil and then allow to cool.

3 Beat the eggs in a mixing bowl, using a fork.

4 Add the beaten eggs and the flour to the cooled mixture.

5 Grease the inside of the baking tin with butter.

6 Place the mixture in the baking tin and bake for 75 minutes.

7 Cool on a wire rack before eating.

Oven-Baked Yams *
(serves 4)

---

2 large yams (or sweet potatoes)
1/4 teaspoon black pepper
3/4 teaspoon salt
3 tablespoons vegetable oil

Utensils: potato peeler, chopping board, kitchen
knife, baking pan (or shallow tray)

Preheat the oven to gas mark 7/220°C/425°F

---

1   Peel the yams using the potato peeler. Cut each
    into sticks 1/2 inch thick and 3 to 4 inches long
    on a chopping board using a kitchen knife –
    ! watch fingers.

2   Grease the pan. Place the yam sticks in the pan
    and toss with the oil, salt and pepper. Spread out
    in one even layer on the bottom of the pan.

3   Bake for 30 minutes until the yams are tender,
    stirring occasionally.

Easy Sauces

Easy White Sauce *

$1^{1}/_{2}$ oz /40g butter
1oz/25g plain flour
$^{3}/_{4}$ pint/425ml milk – must be cold
salt and pepper

Utensils: saucepan, balloon whisk, wooden spoon,
measuring jug

1 Put all the ingredients into a saucepan and place on a medium heat.

2 Whisk until the sauce begins to bubble.

3 Stir the sauce with a wooden spoon and reduce the heat until it's as low as possible.

4 Simmer gently for 5 minutes, stirring now and again.

   (It is important to whisk and stir all the time until the sauce has boiled – otherwise it will be lumpy).

Easy French Dressing *
(dresses 1 large salad)

Made with white wine vinegar and olive oil, this is the perfect dressing for a green salad. Or pour over hot new potatoes for a tasty and healthy change from butter.

---

1 tablespoon white wine vinegar
3 tablespoons olive oil or vegetable oil
1 teaspoon seeded mustard
(Lakeshore or Dalkey is ideal)
large pinch of salt and pepper

Utensils: mixing bowl and metal spoon

---

1 Place all the ingredients in a bowl and mix together.

Easy Curry Sauce *

---

1 carton of cottage cheese
1 packet of Philadelphia cream cheese
1 teaspoon curry powder
3 tablespoons mayonnaise

---

1 Place all the ingredients in a food processor and 'whoosh' together until creamy.
2 Serve with crisps, Pringles or cut vegetable sticks.

Easy American Chocolate Sauce *

4oz/110g plain chocolate
$^1/_2$ pint/175ml water
1oz/25g caster sugar

Utensils: 2 saucepans, metal spoon, small bowl

---

1 Boil the sugar and the water in a saucepan for 5 minutes.

2 Break the chocolate into pieces and place in a small bowl. Place the bowl over a saucepan of gently boiling water. Make sure no water gets into the chocolate at this stage.

3 Once the chocolate is melted add the sugar and water syrup, spoon by spoon. Beat well after each added spoon. The sauce will get smoother as you add the syrup and stir.

4 Serve hot or cold over ice-cream or fruit.

Easy Fried Rice *
(serves 4)

---

2 onions
3 celery sticks
2 red peppers
1 lb/450g long-grained rice
8oz/225g frozen peas
salt and pepper
3 tablespoons oil

Utensils: chopping board, sharp knife, large
frying pan or wok, spatula, 2 saucepans, drainer,
metal spoon

---

1 Cook the rice, following the packet instructions.

2 Place the peas in a saucepan and cook, following
packet instructions. Drain and put aside.

3 Chop the onions and slice the celery – *! watch
fingers.*

4 Cut the peppers in half and remove the seeds and
pulp. Cut into pieces – *! watch fingers.*

5 Heat the oil in the frying pan or wok. Add the
onions and fry until soft.

6 Add the celery and red pepper and fry for 5
minutes.

7 Stir in the rice and peas and season with a pinch
of salt and pepper. Heat gently until warm.

Easy Sweet and Sour Barbecue Sauce *
(makes $1/2$ pint)

---

2 tablespoons sugar
4 tablespoons tomato chutney
1 tablespoon Worcester sauce
1 clove of garlic chopped
2 tablespoons white wine vinegar
$1/2$ teaspoon mustard
1 tablespoon mixed herbs
1 tablespoon chopped onions
2oz/50g butter
1 tablespoon water

Utensils: large saucepan, wooden spoon,
serving dish

---

1 Place the ingredients in a saucepan and cook on a
   low heat until boiling (about 15 minutes).

2 Simmer for 5 minutes until thickened.

3 Serve with chicken or pork.

After you finish

1) Make sure the cooker is switched off and any electrical machines are off and unplugged.
2) Put away any leftover ingredients. Milk, eggs, cheese and meat must be put back in the fridge, along with any other food that might go off.
3) Wash and dry all the dirty utensils and put them away. This is the un-fun bit! But you could get a friend or parent to help, maybe even a little sister or brother.
4) Clean down the counters and table-tops.
5) Leave everything clean and tidy.

Index

For easy reference, the recipes are in italics

Author

When she's not writing, Sarah Webb works as the marketing manager of children's books for Eason. She lives in a converted coach house in Co Dublin, with her young son, Sam. Sarah was a founding member of Children's Books Ireland and organises children's book events for children and adults.

Kids Can Cook Around the World is her third children's book; the other titles, both published by Children's Press, are *Kids Can Cook* and *Children's Parties*.

She also writes romantic fiction for adults: *Three Times a Lady* and *Always the Bridesmaid* (Poolbeg Press). She appears regularly on RTE's Den 2, demonstrating art, craft and cookery.

In her spare time Sarah loves sailing, reading, cooking and eating. Her favourite foods, depending on her mood, include ice-cream, pasta and pizza.